I0446913

This Book Belongs To...

____

____

____

____

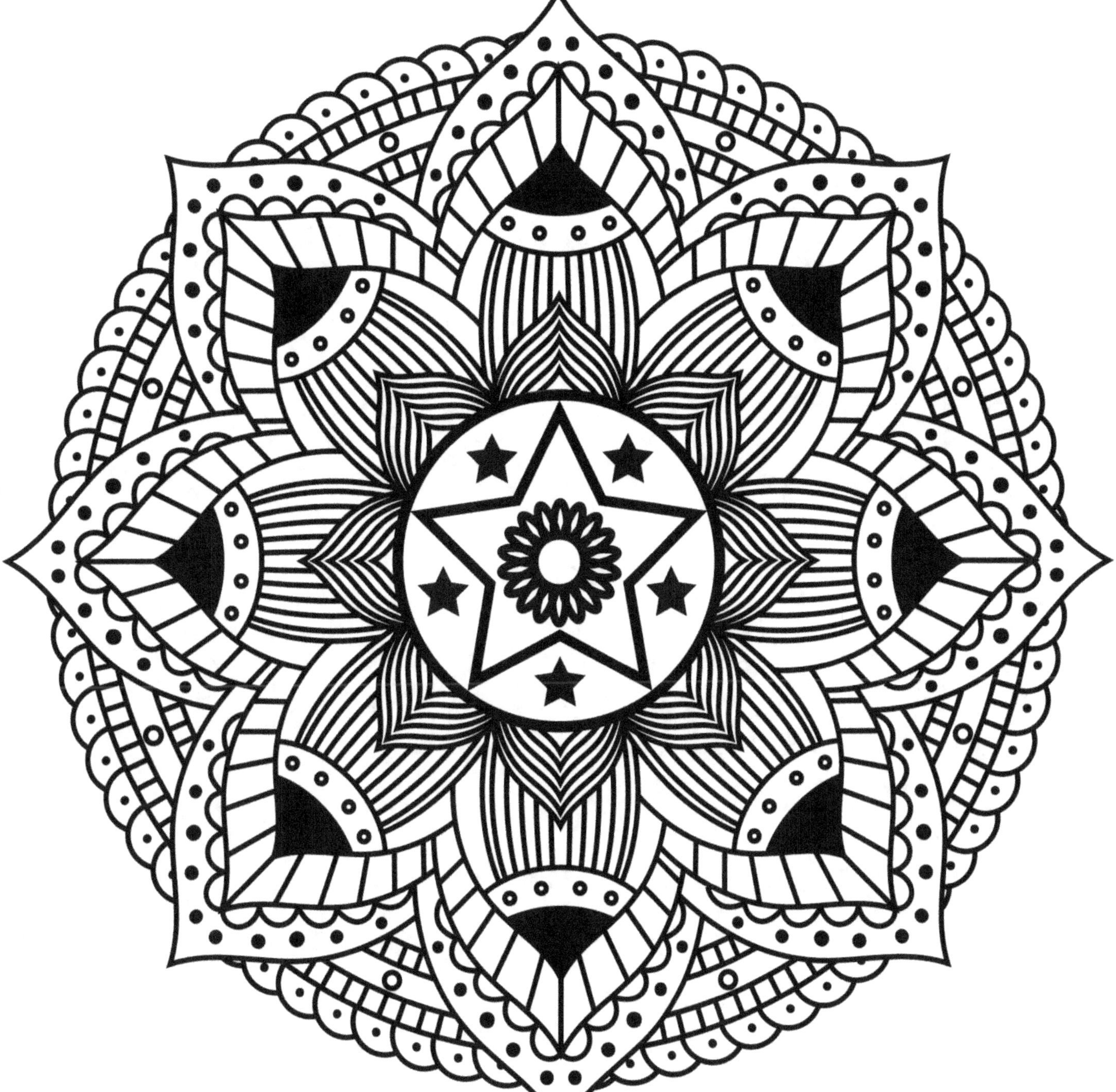

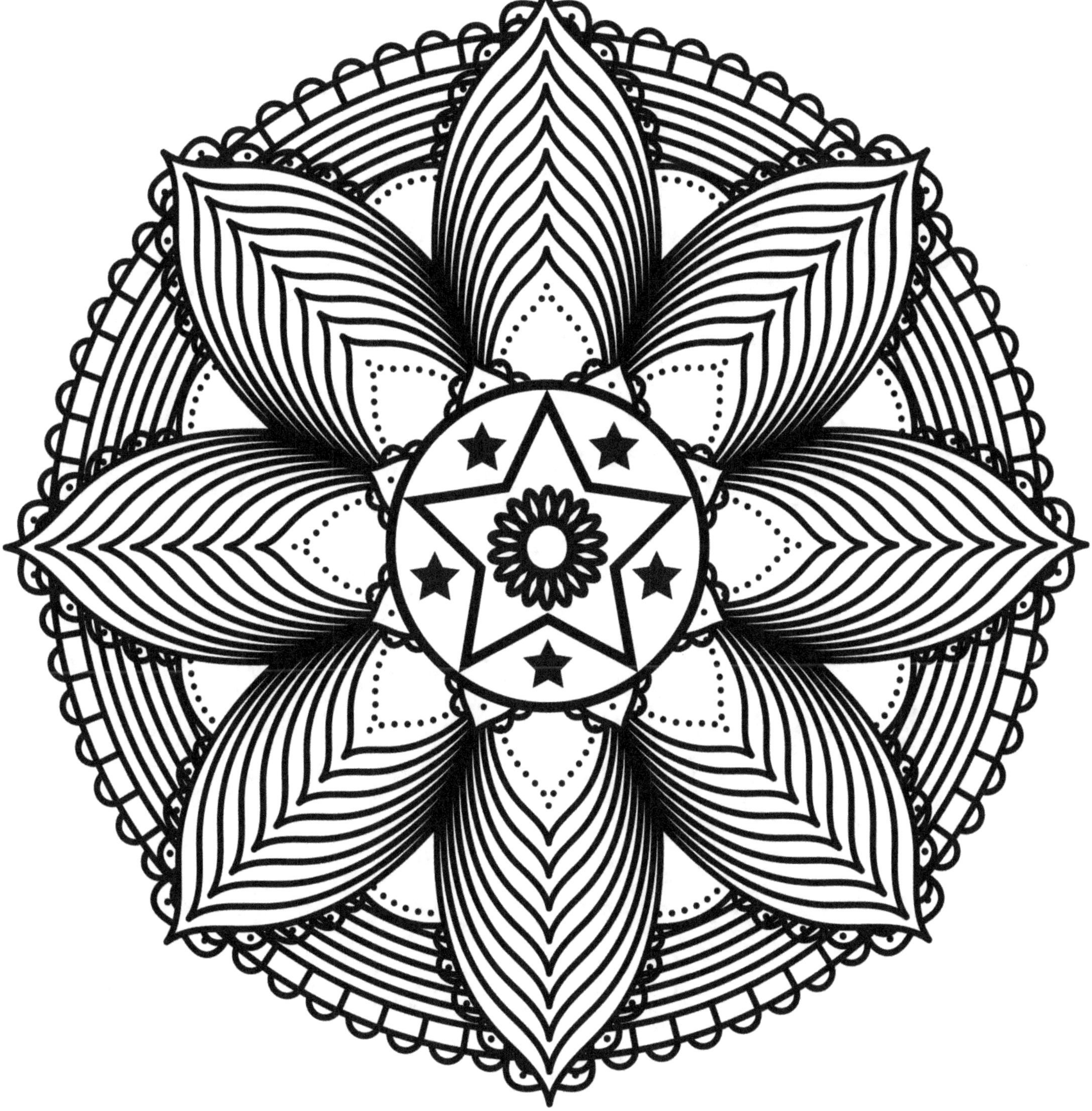

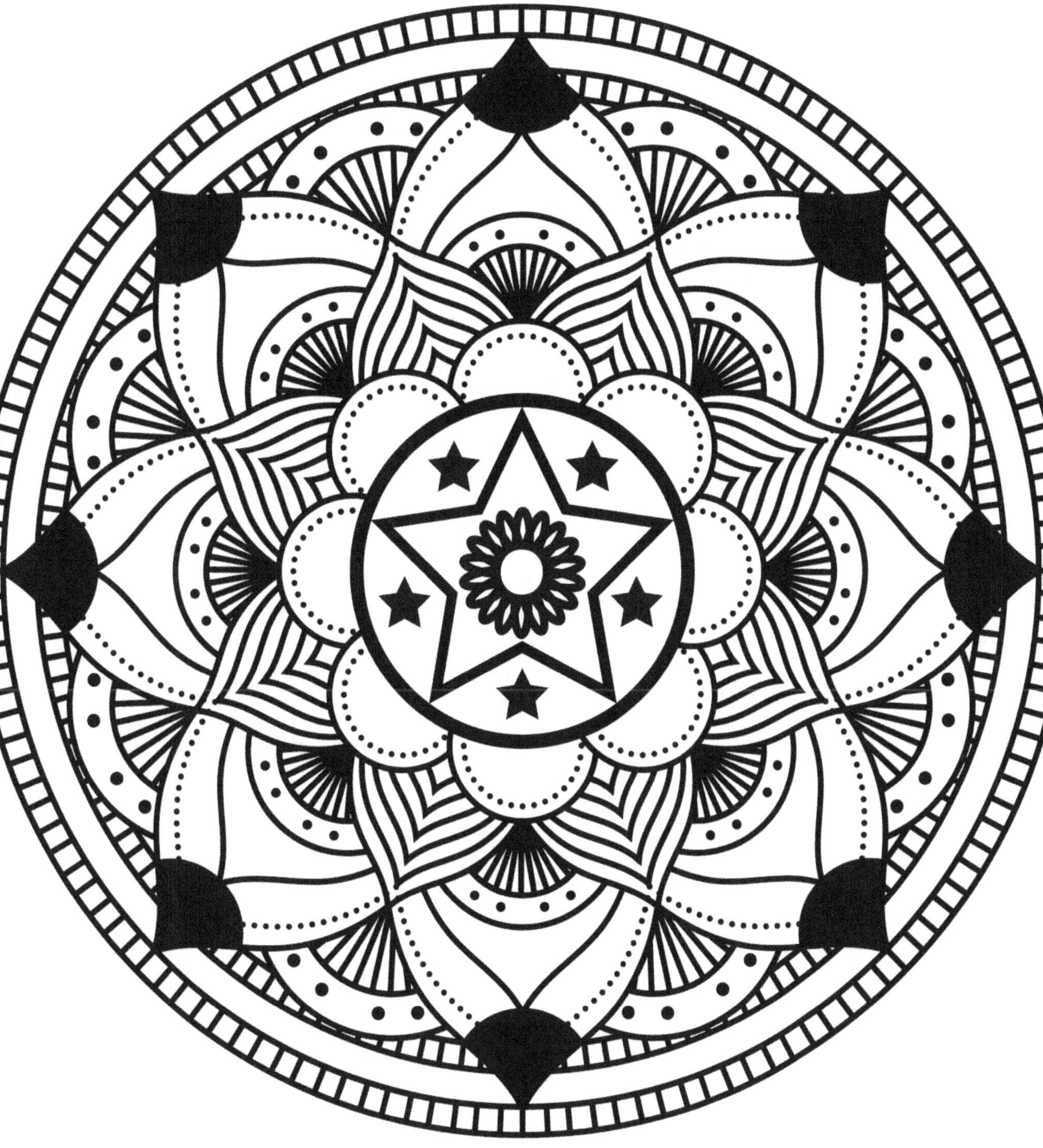

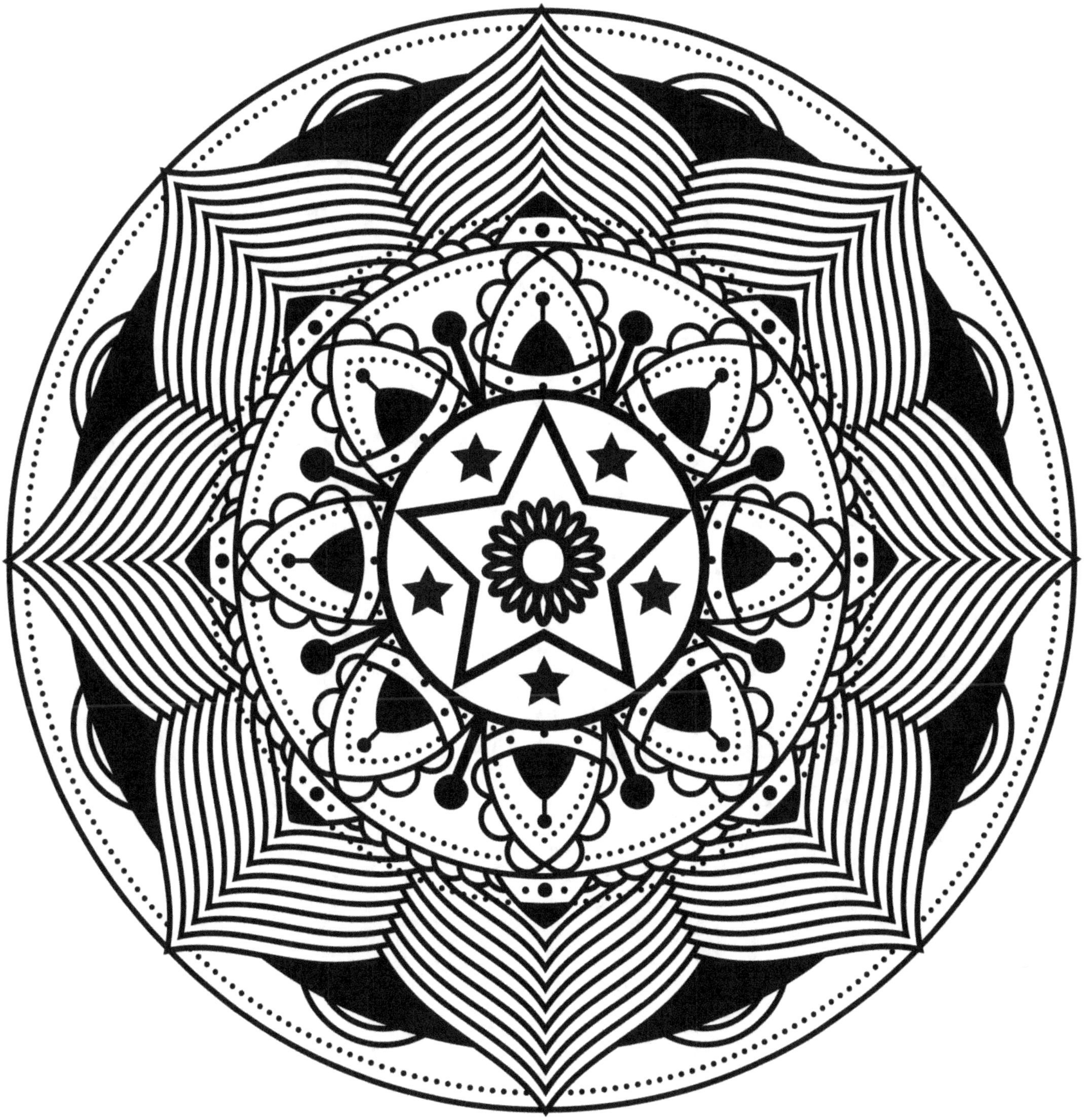

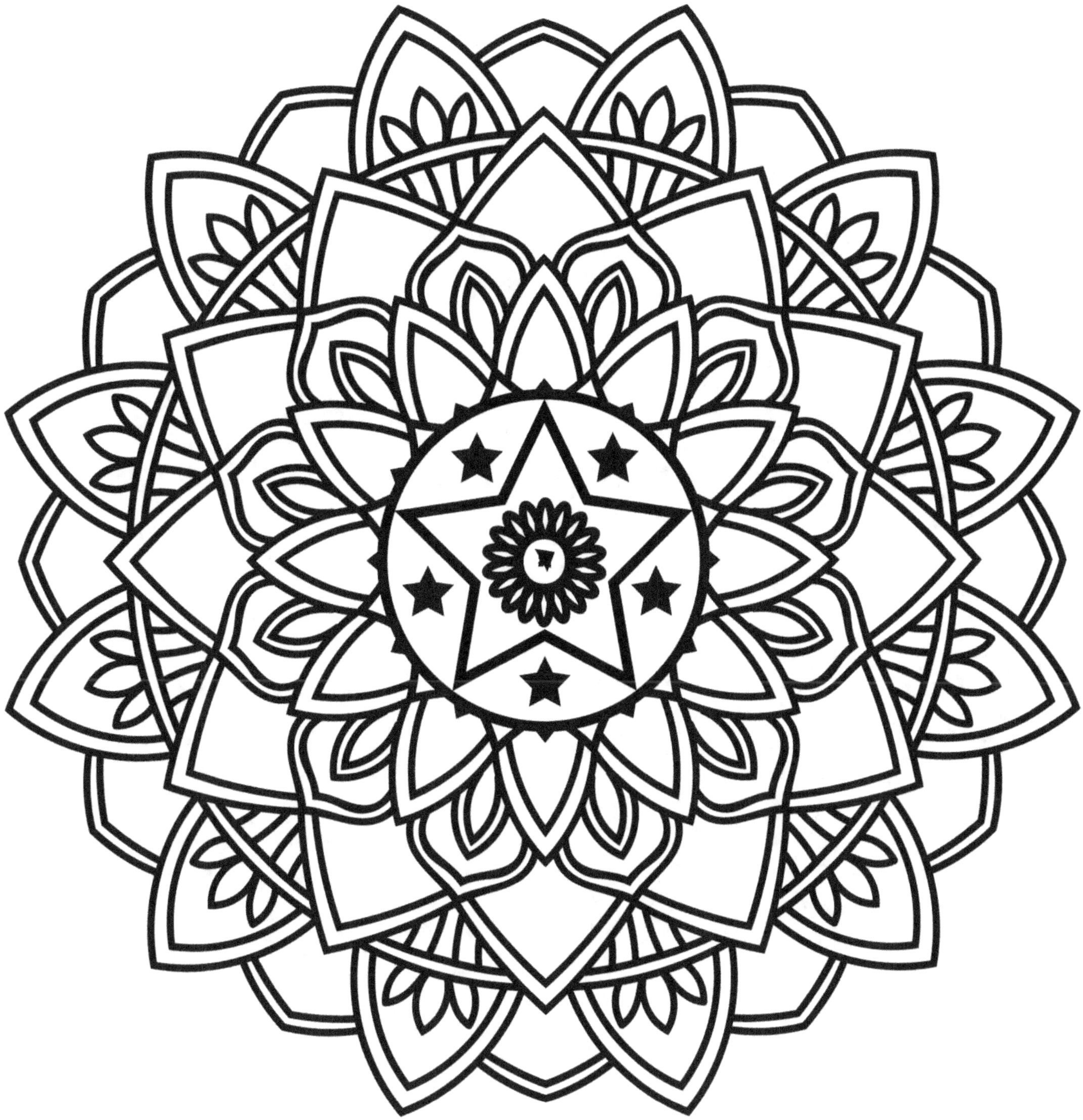

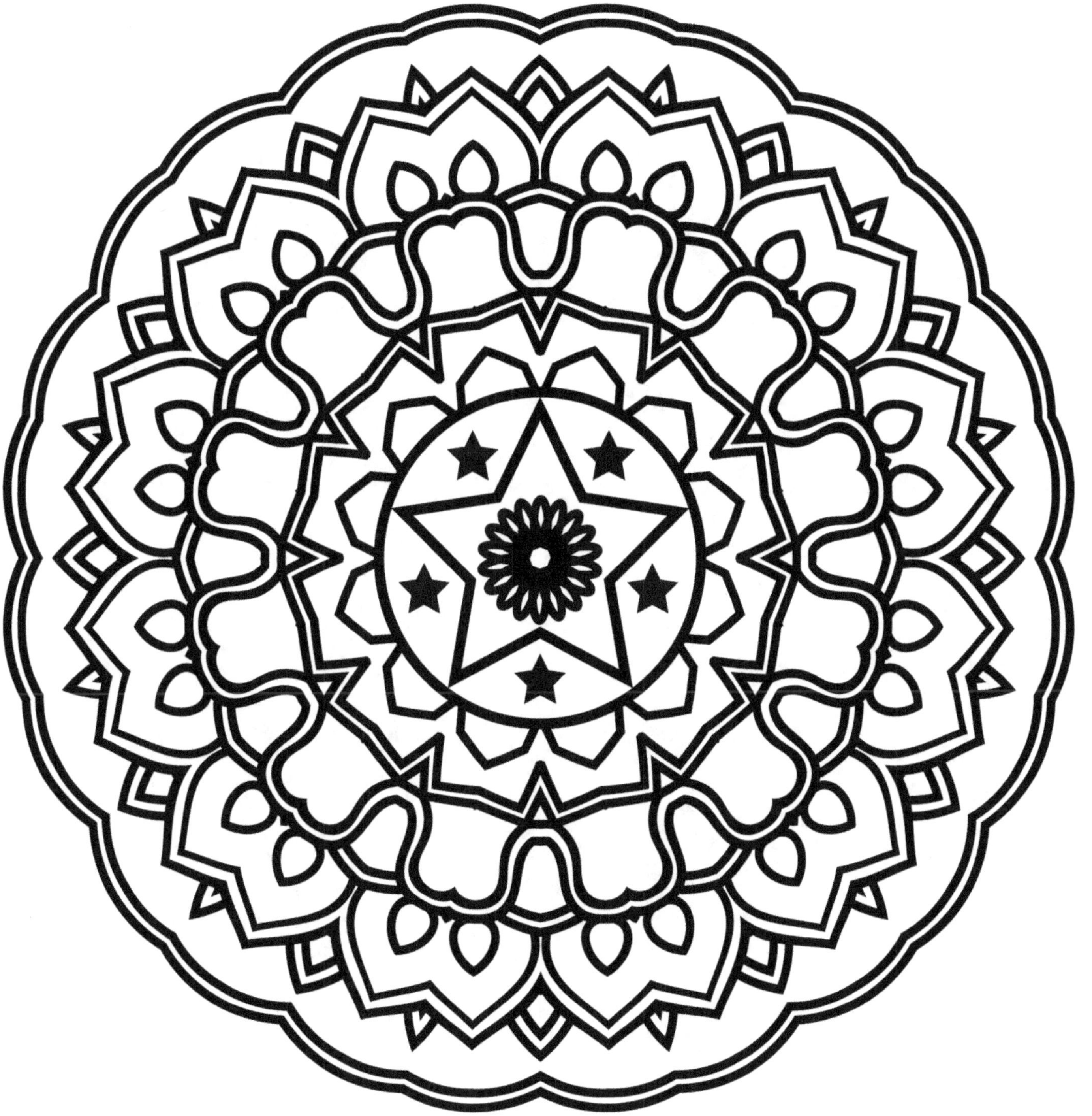

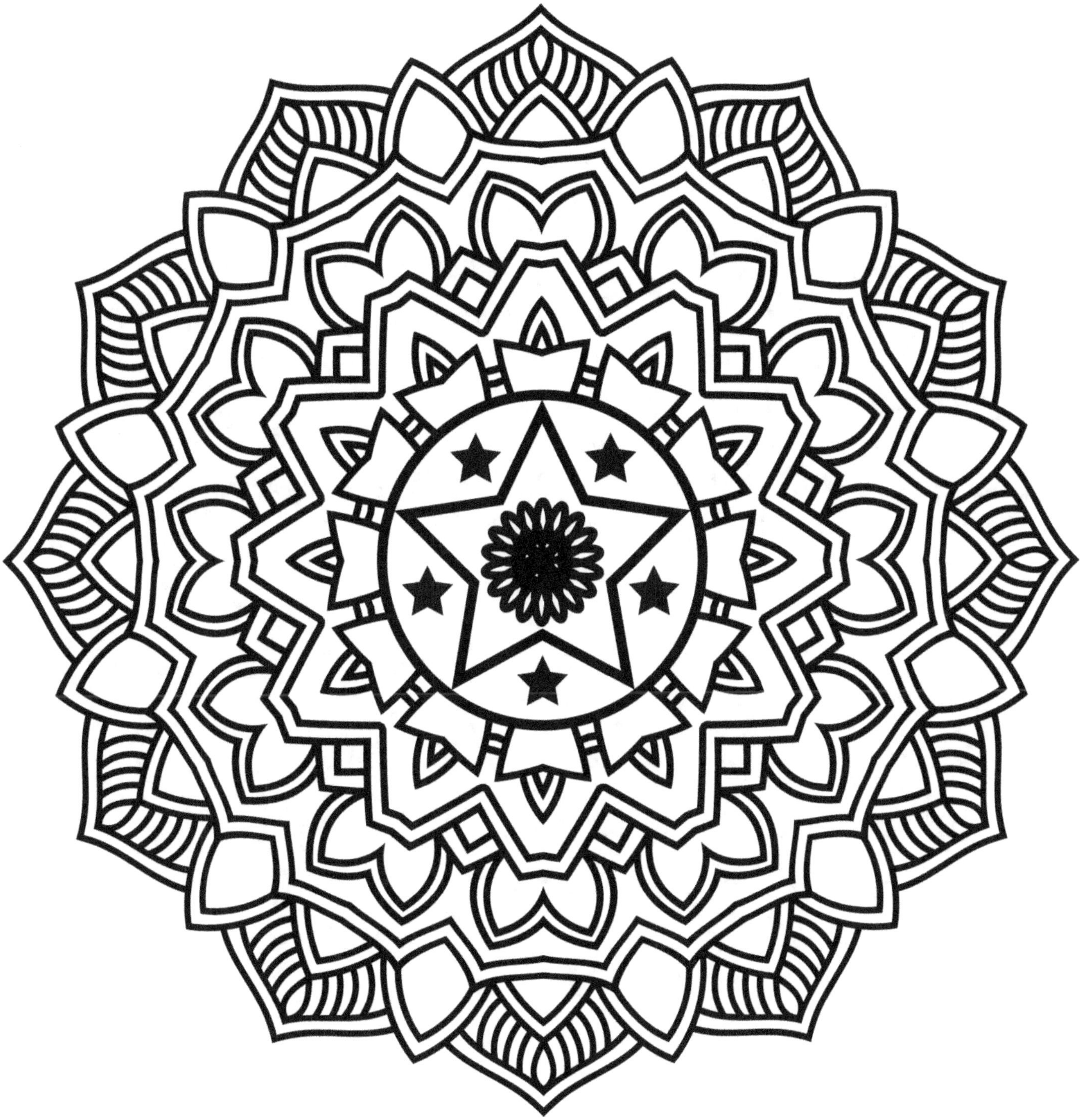

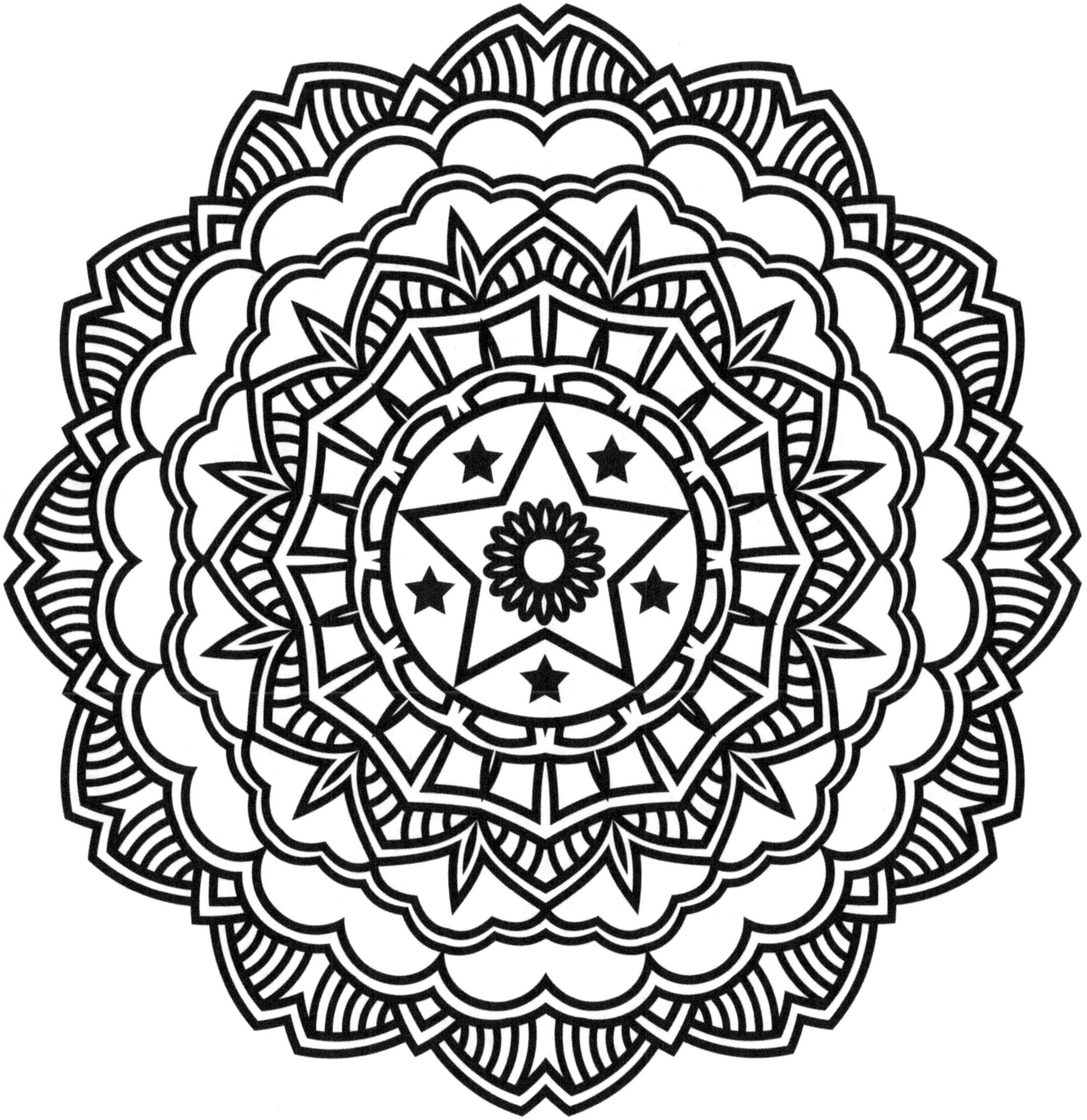

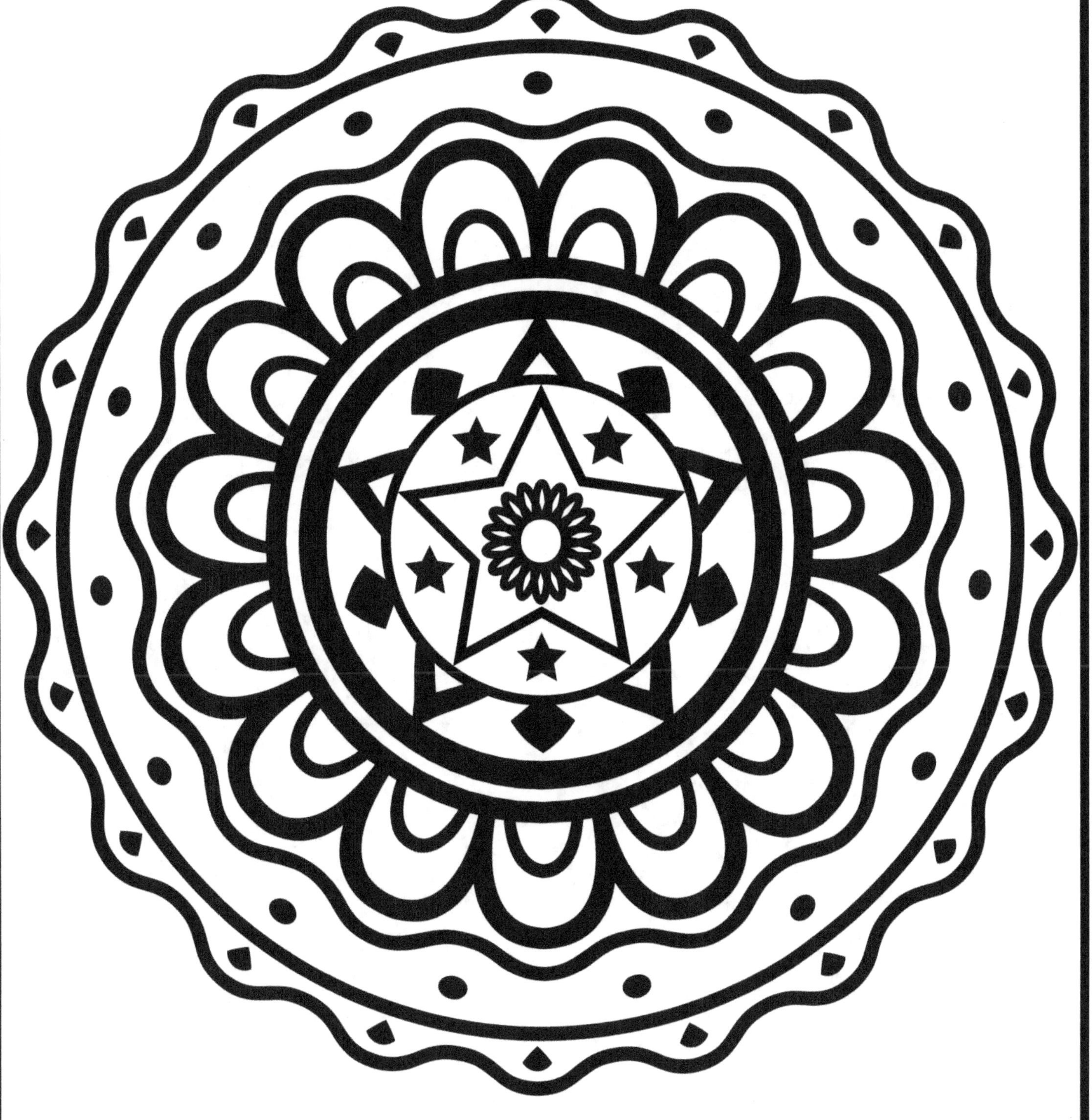

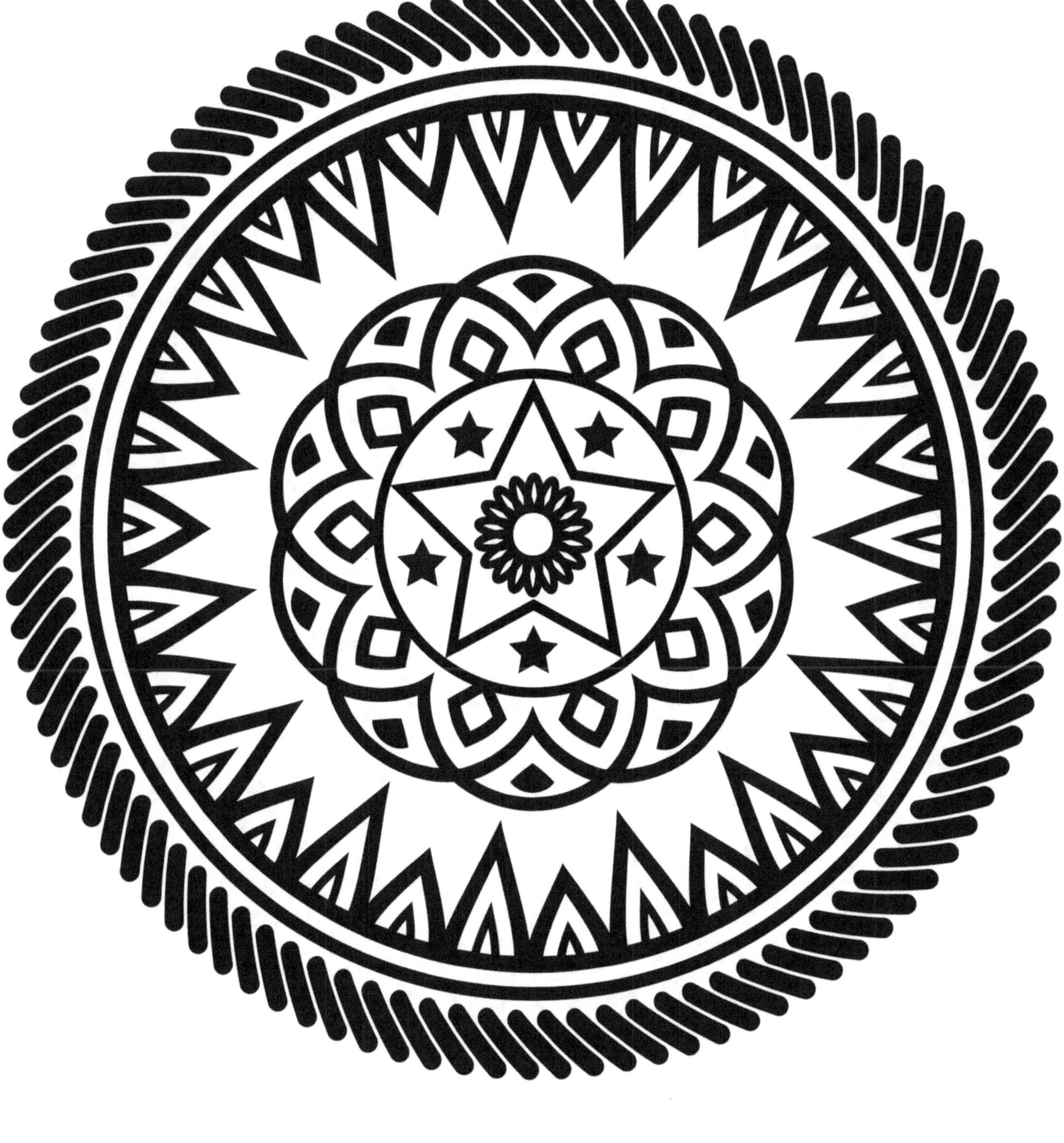

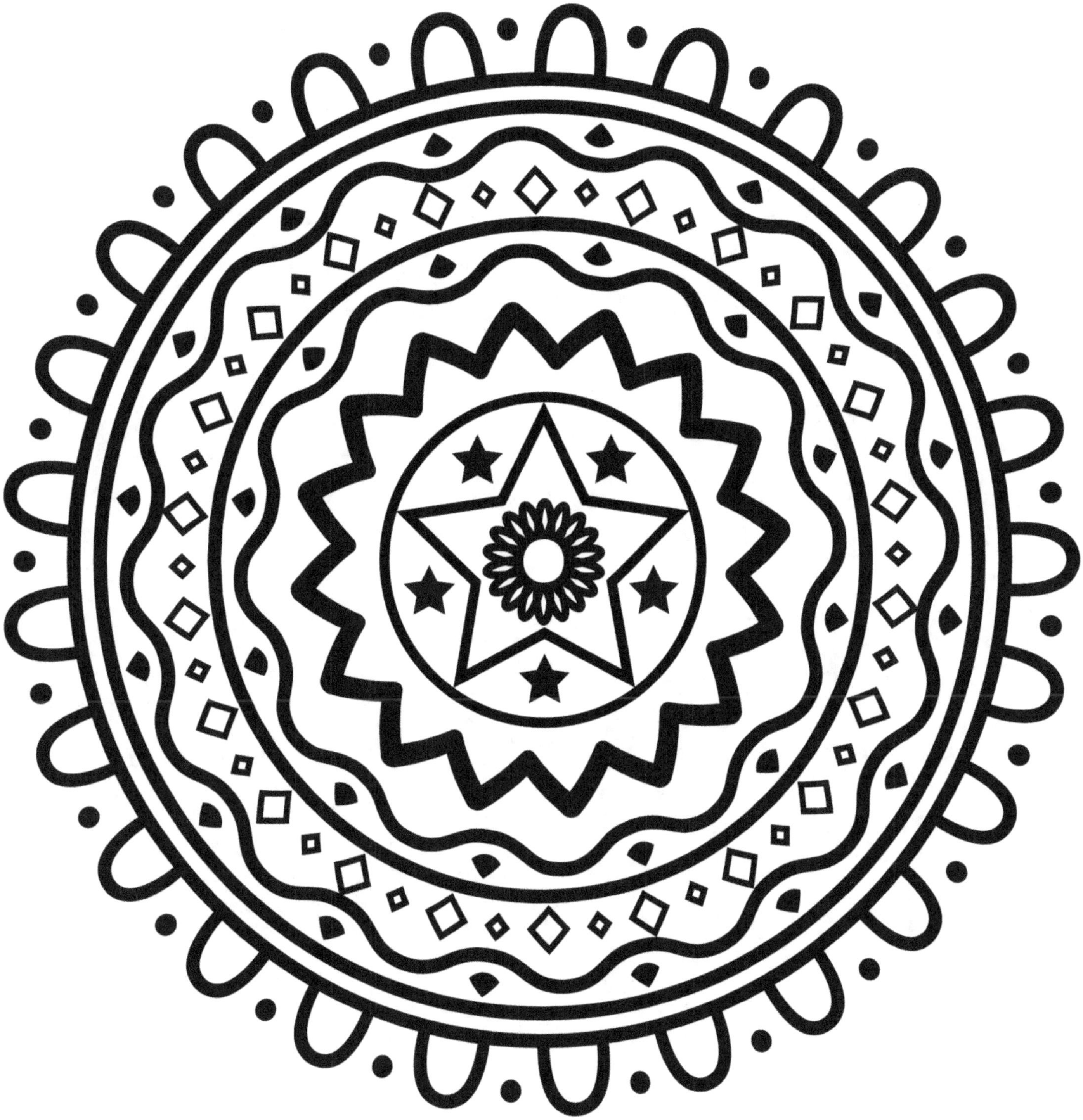

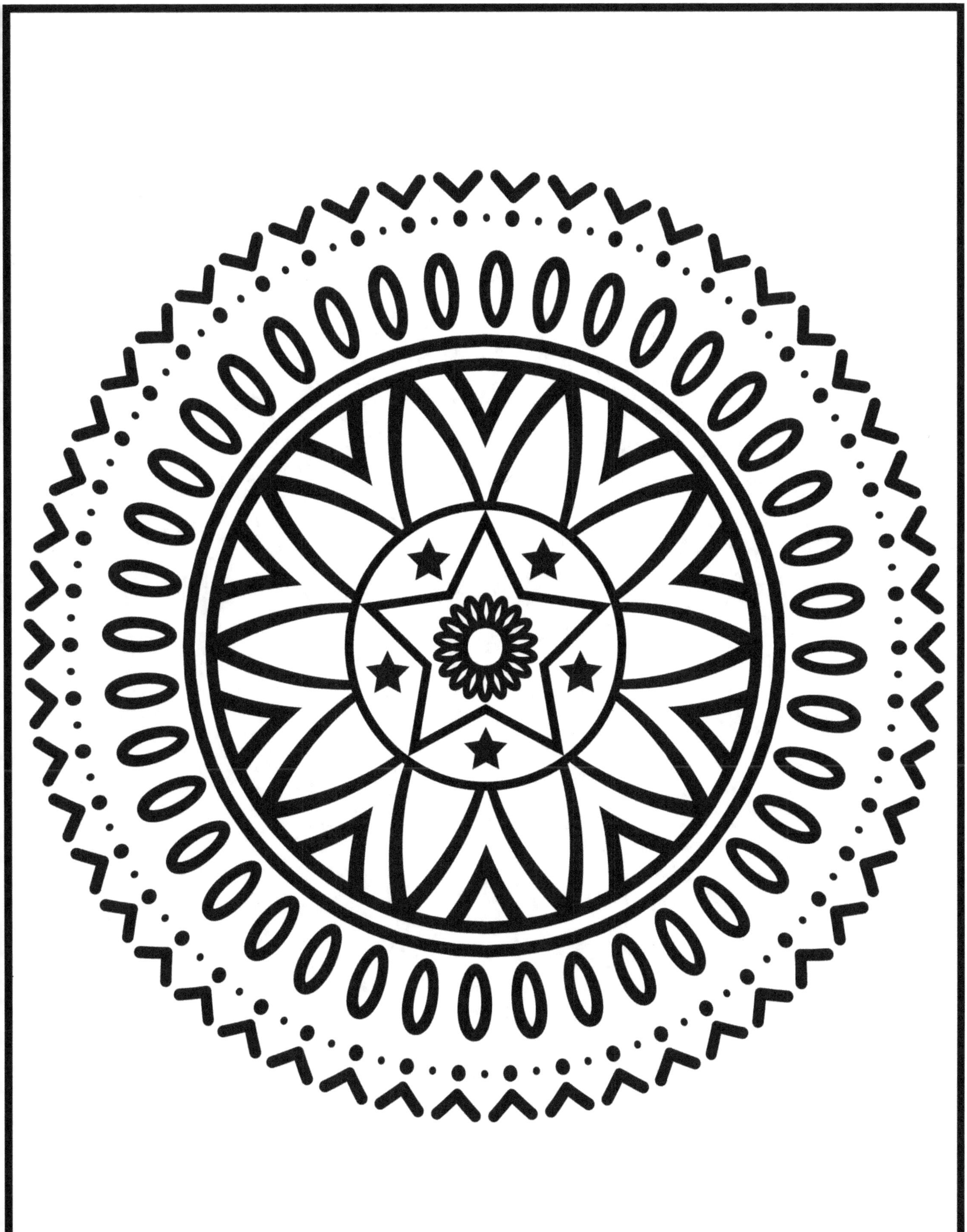

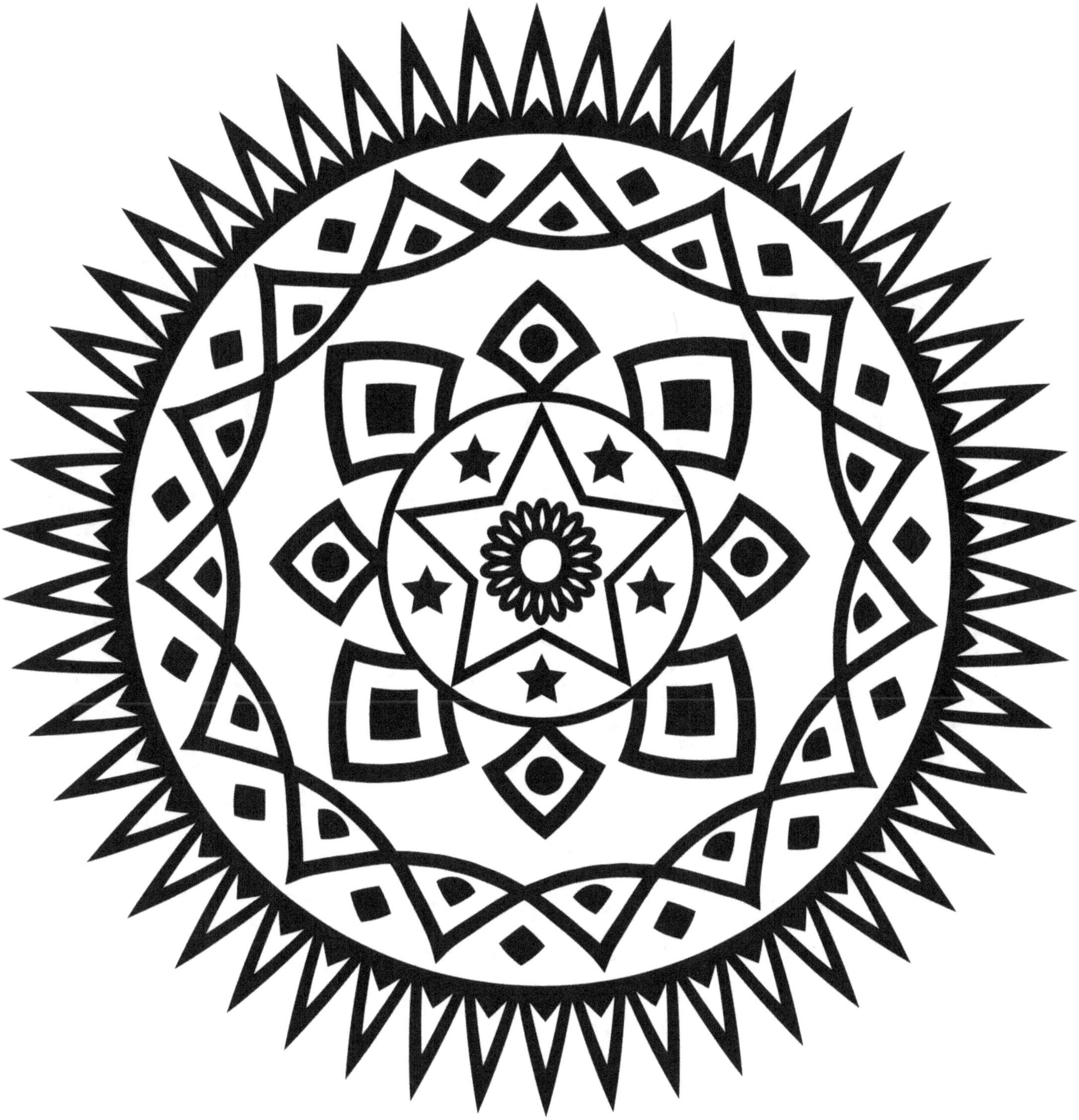

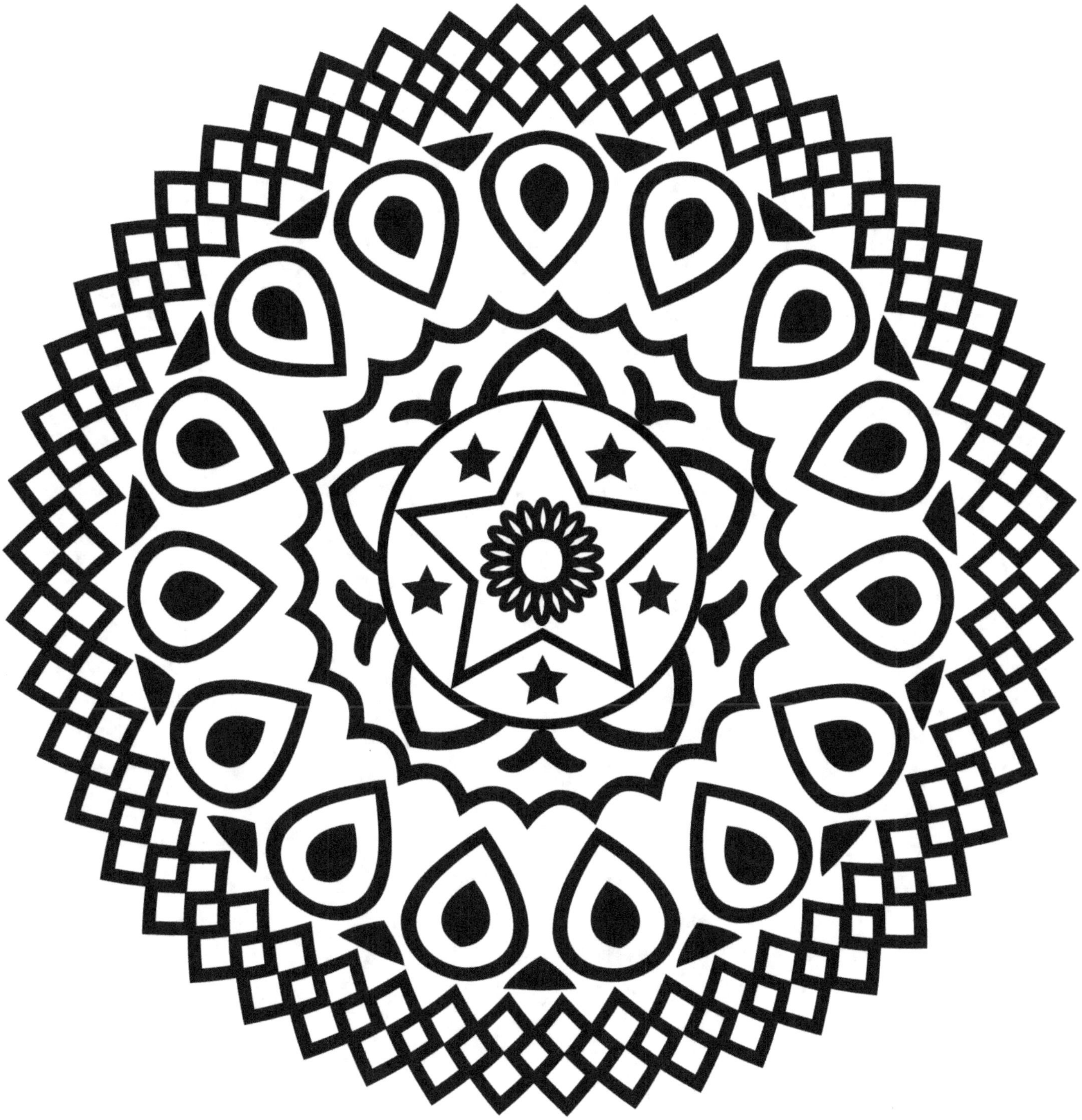

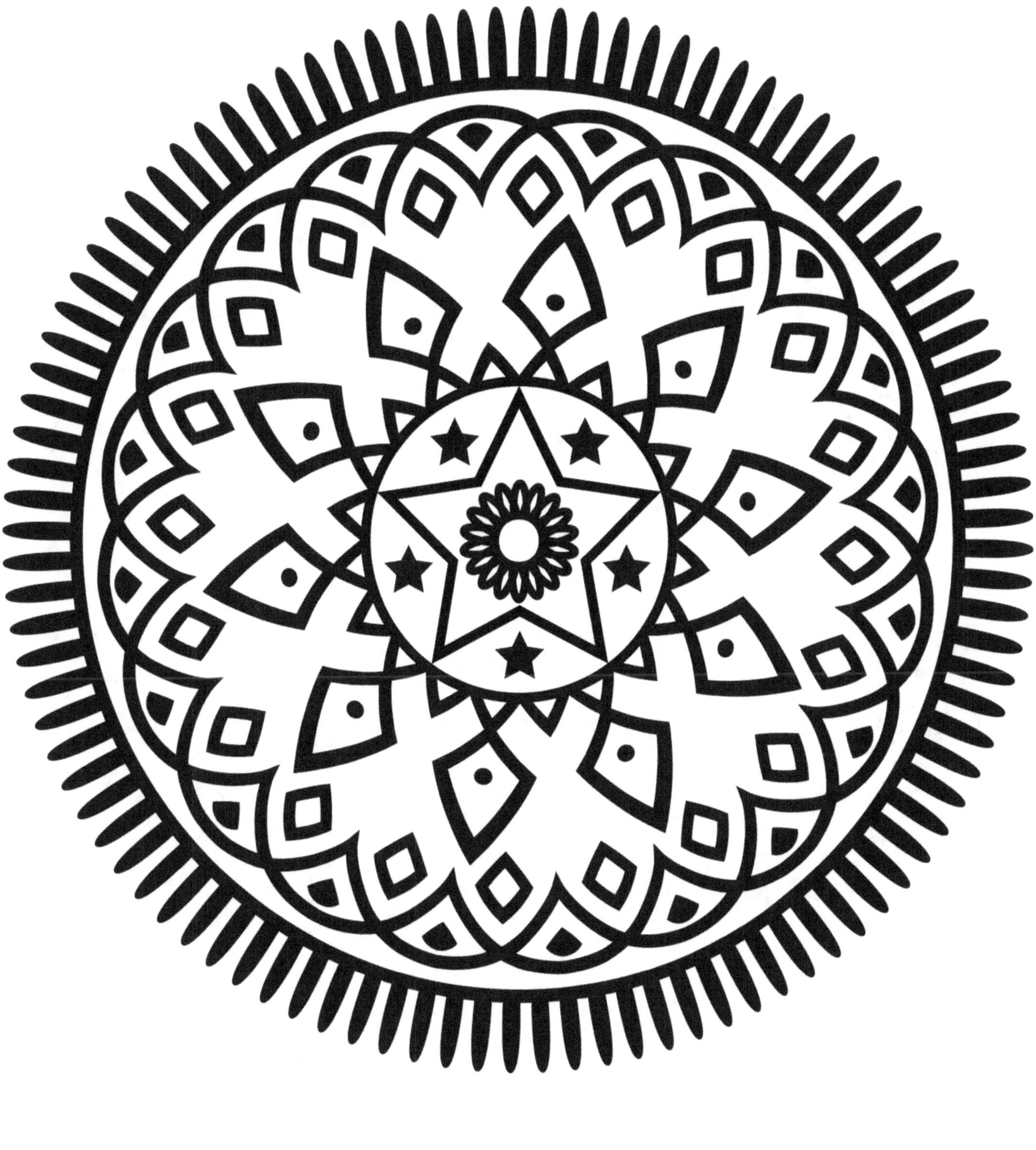

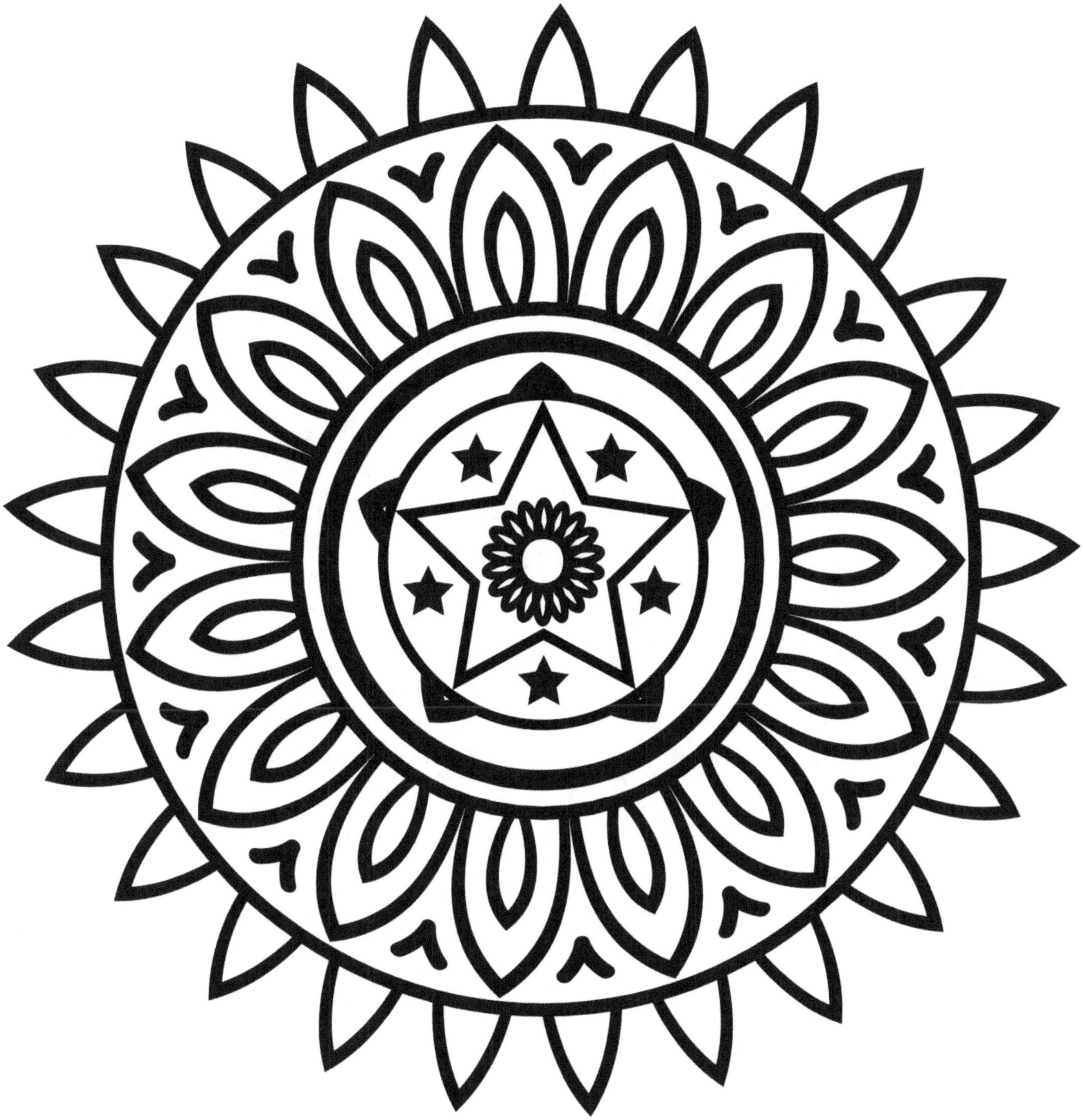

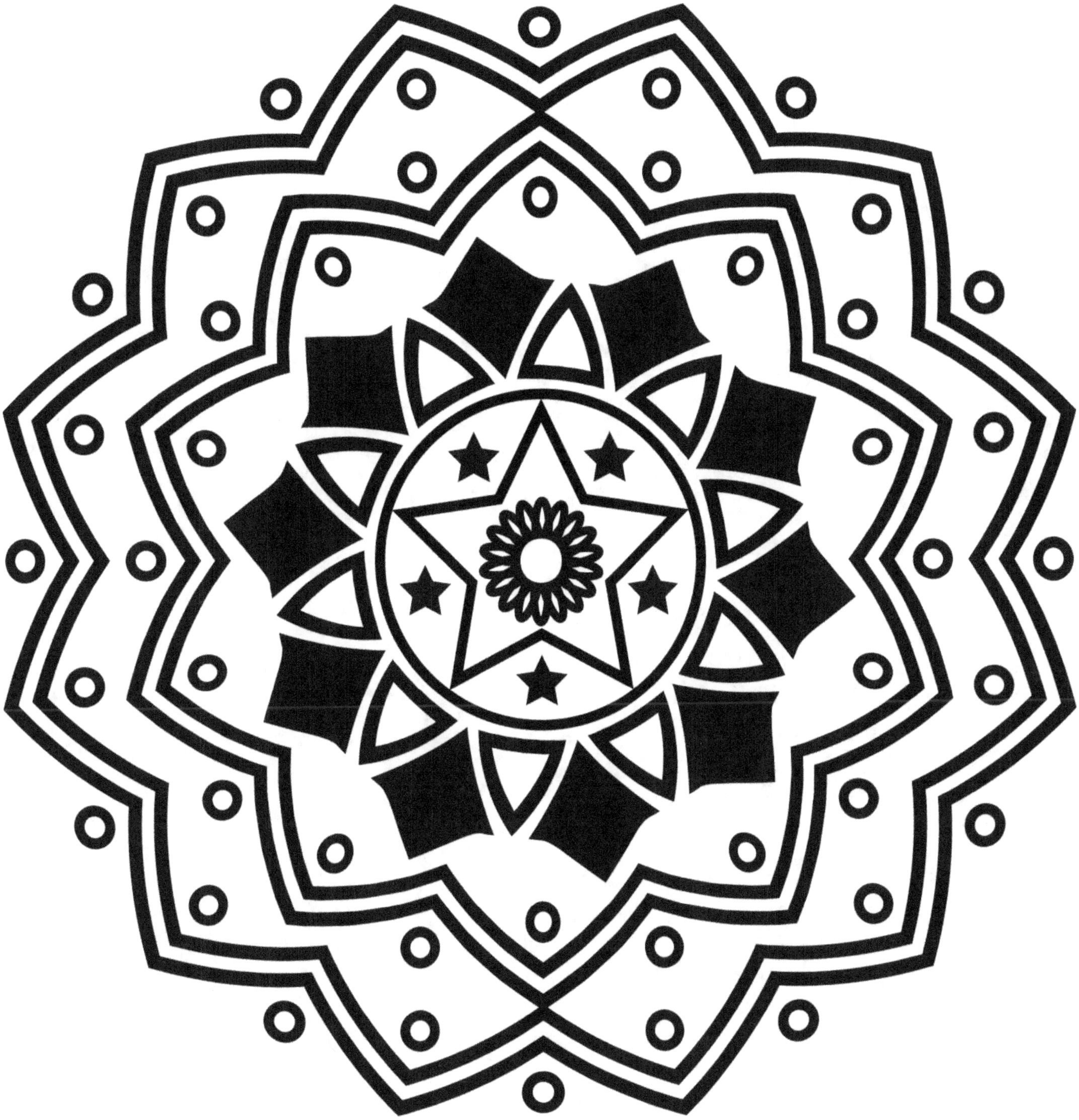

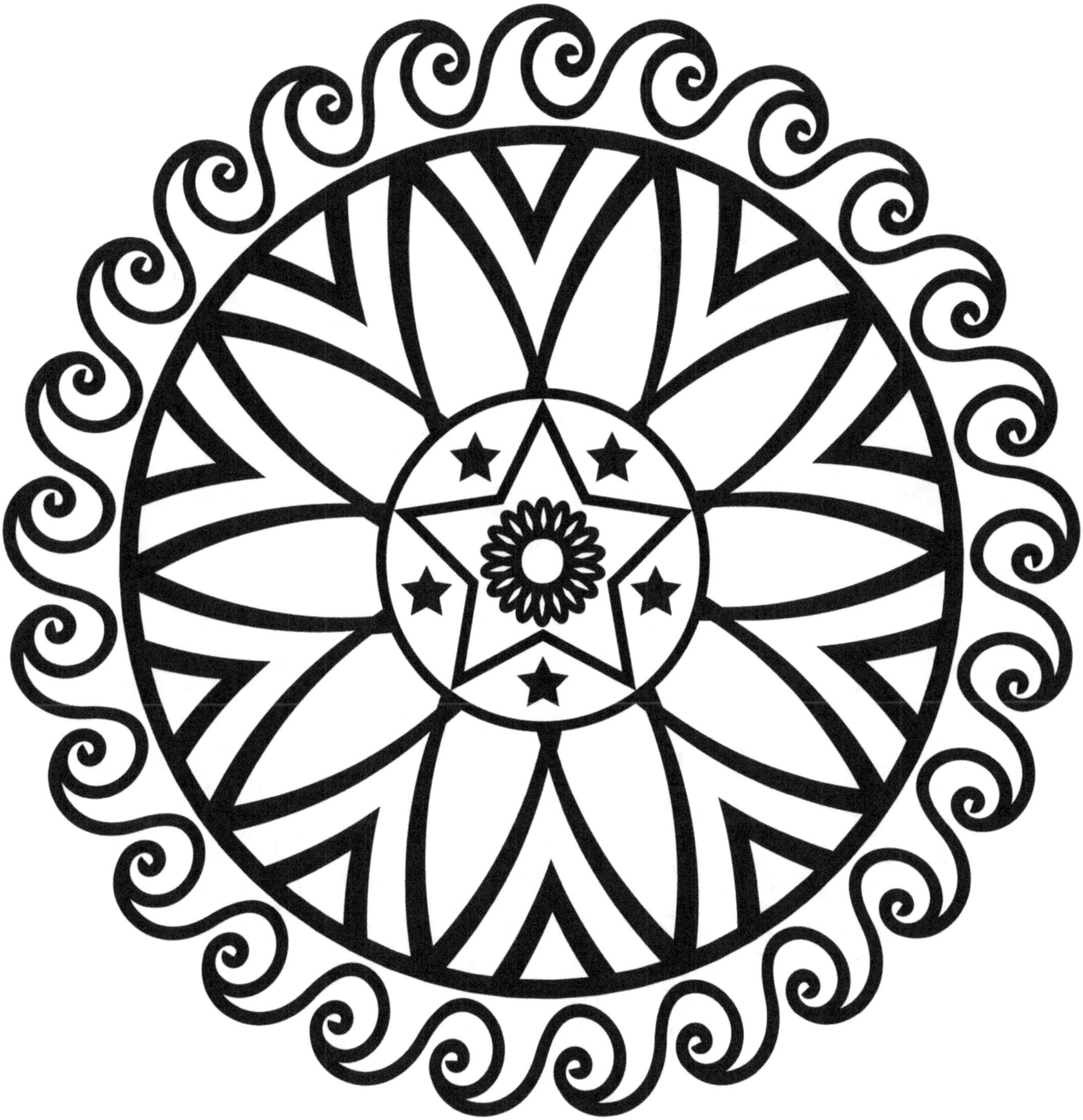

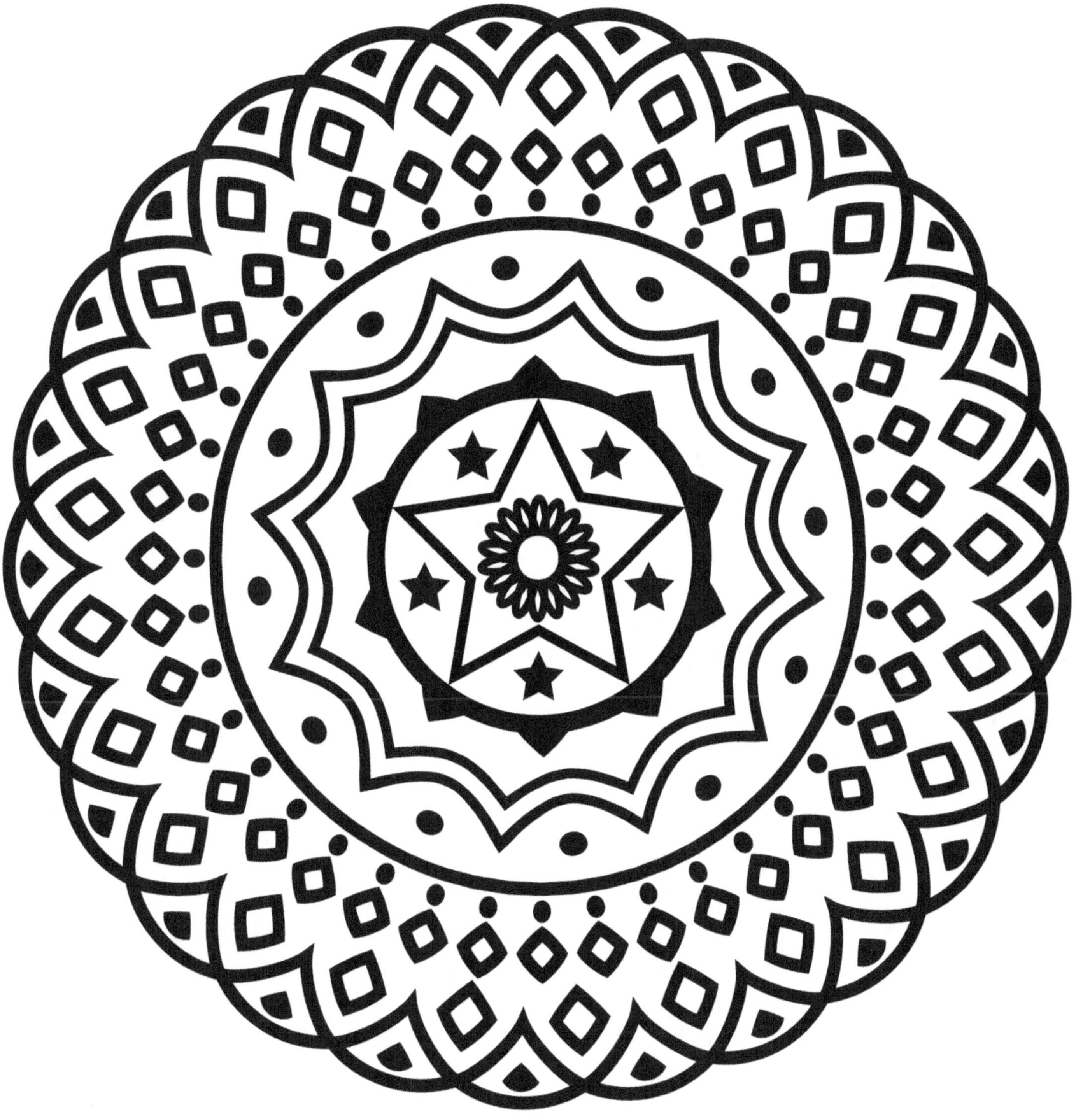

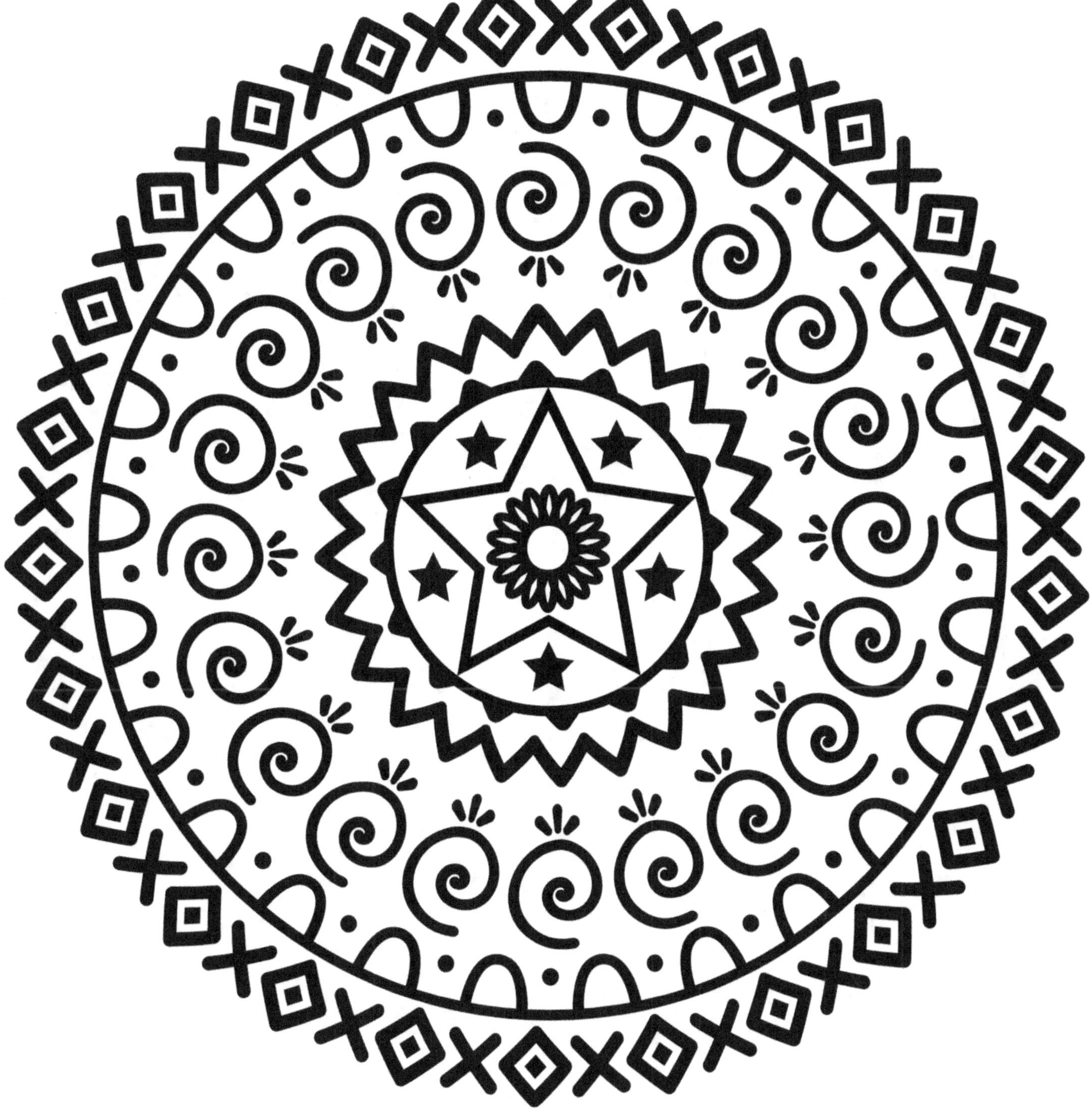

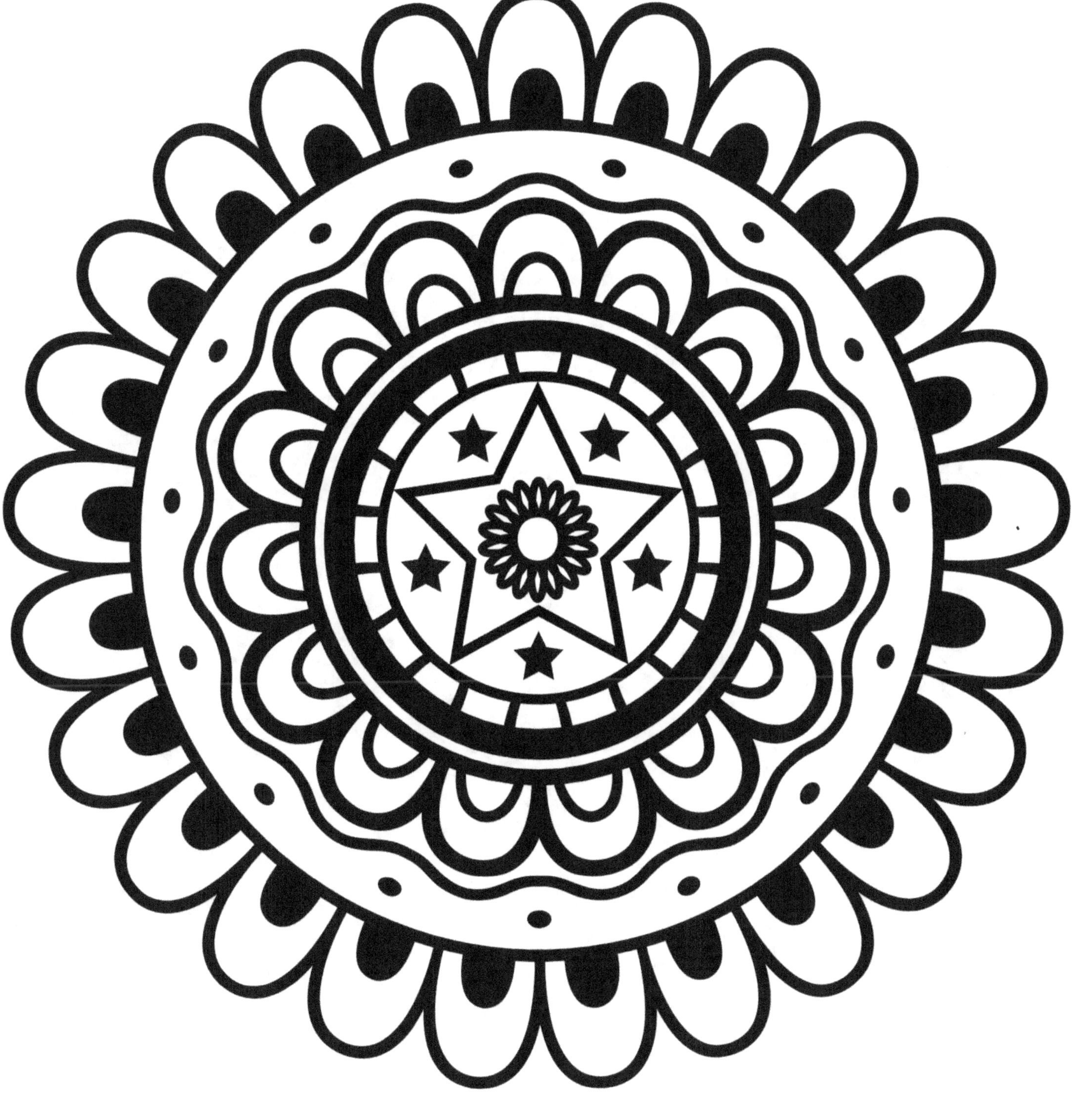

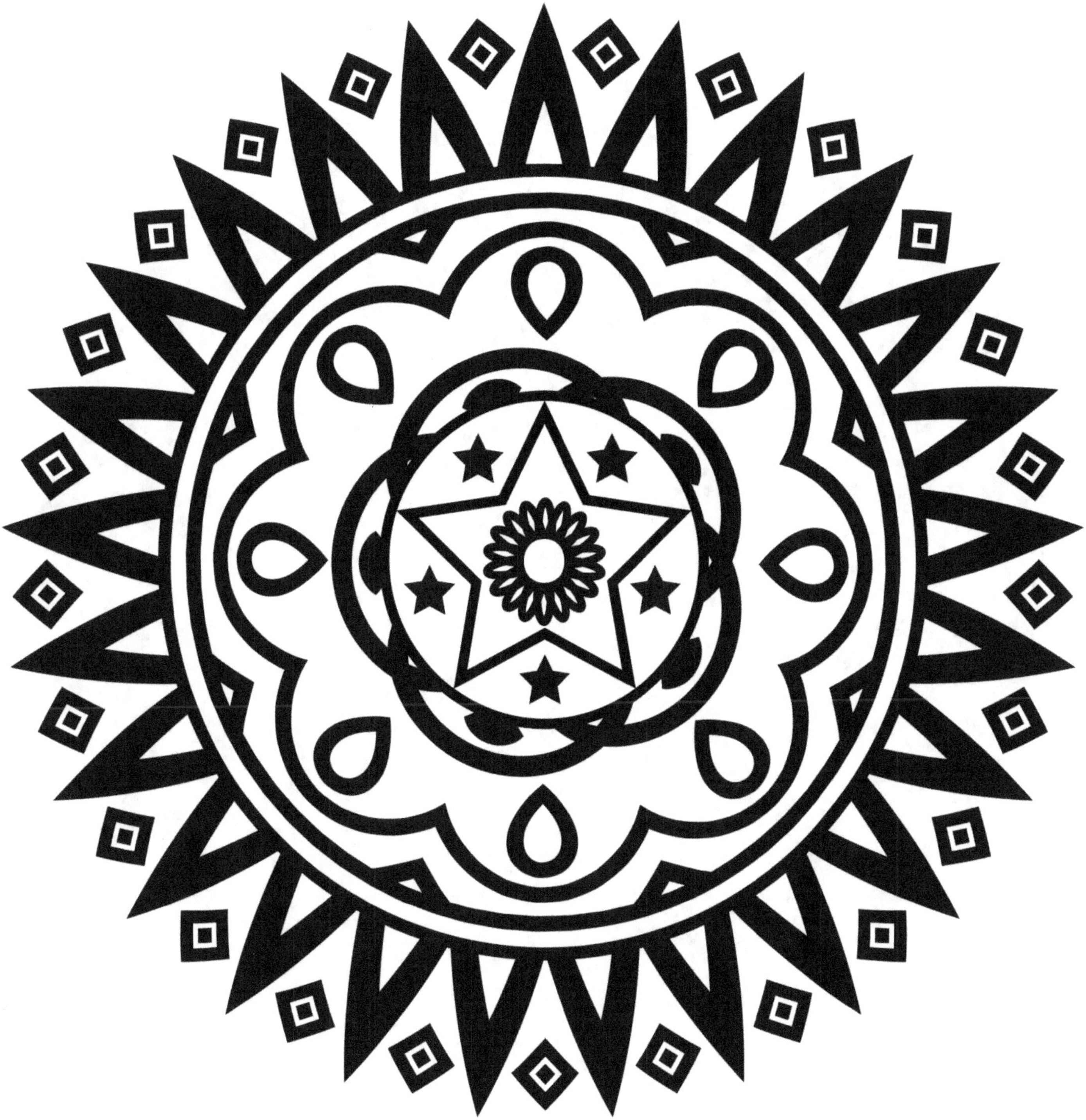

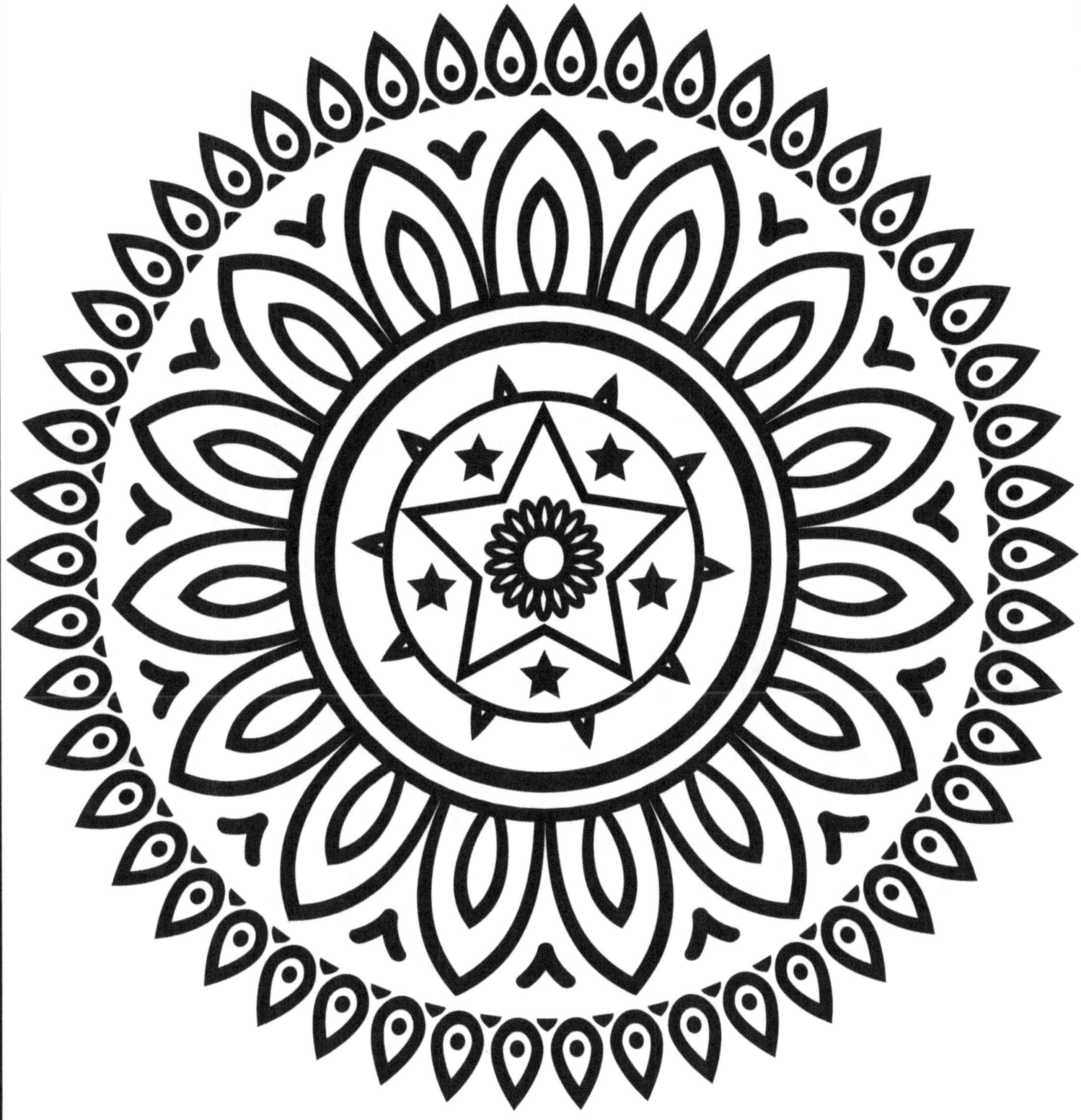

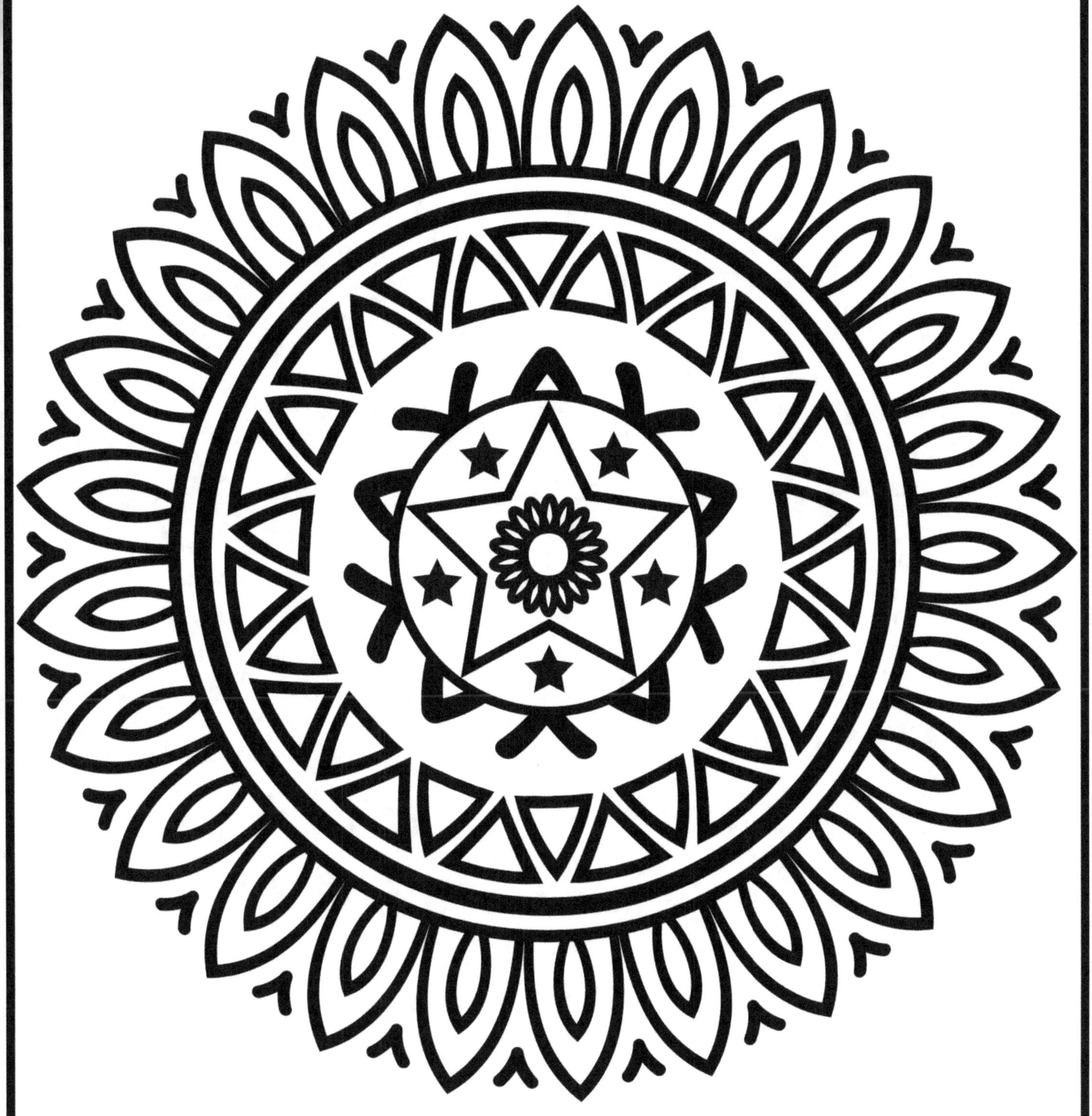

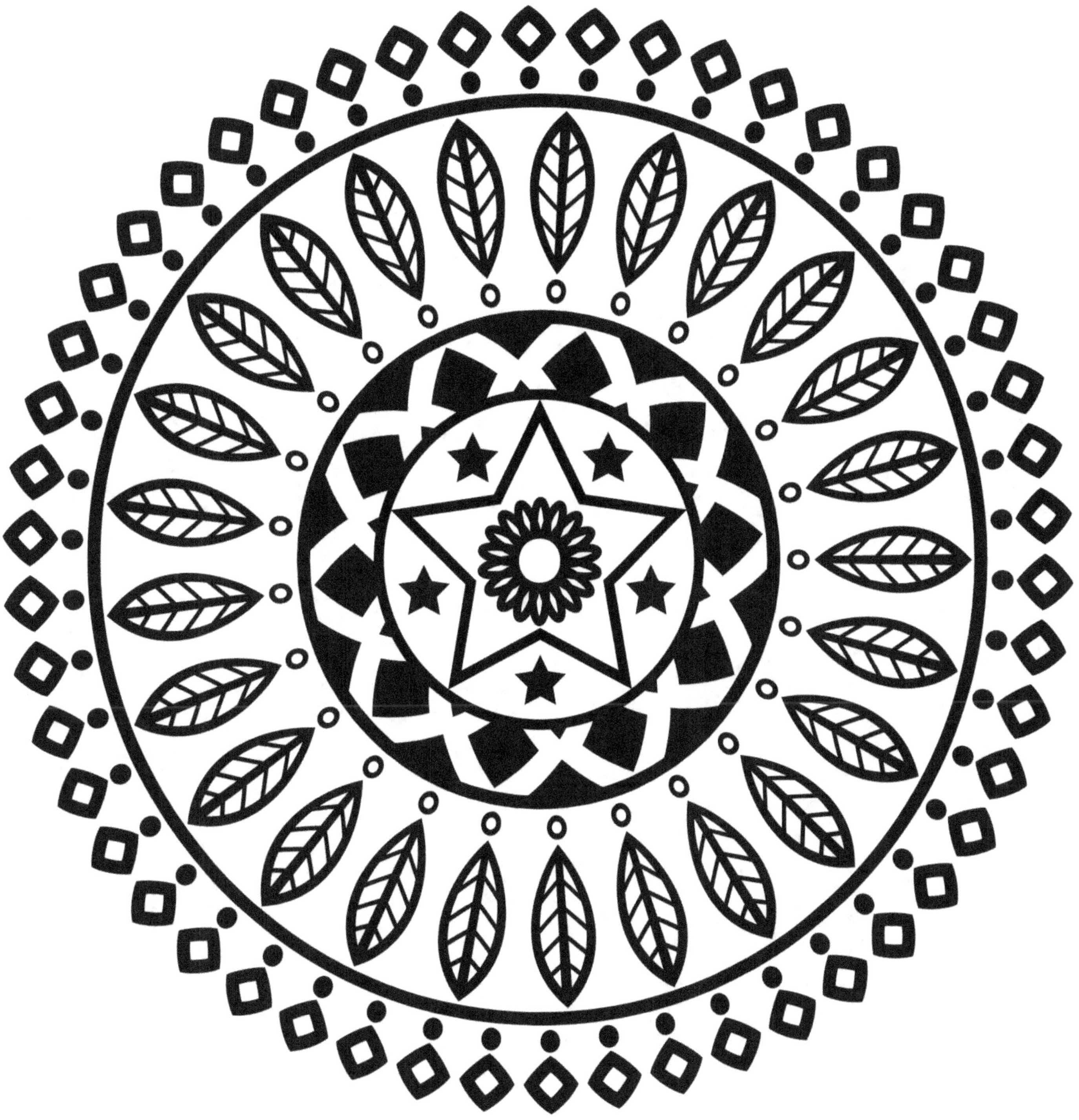

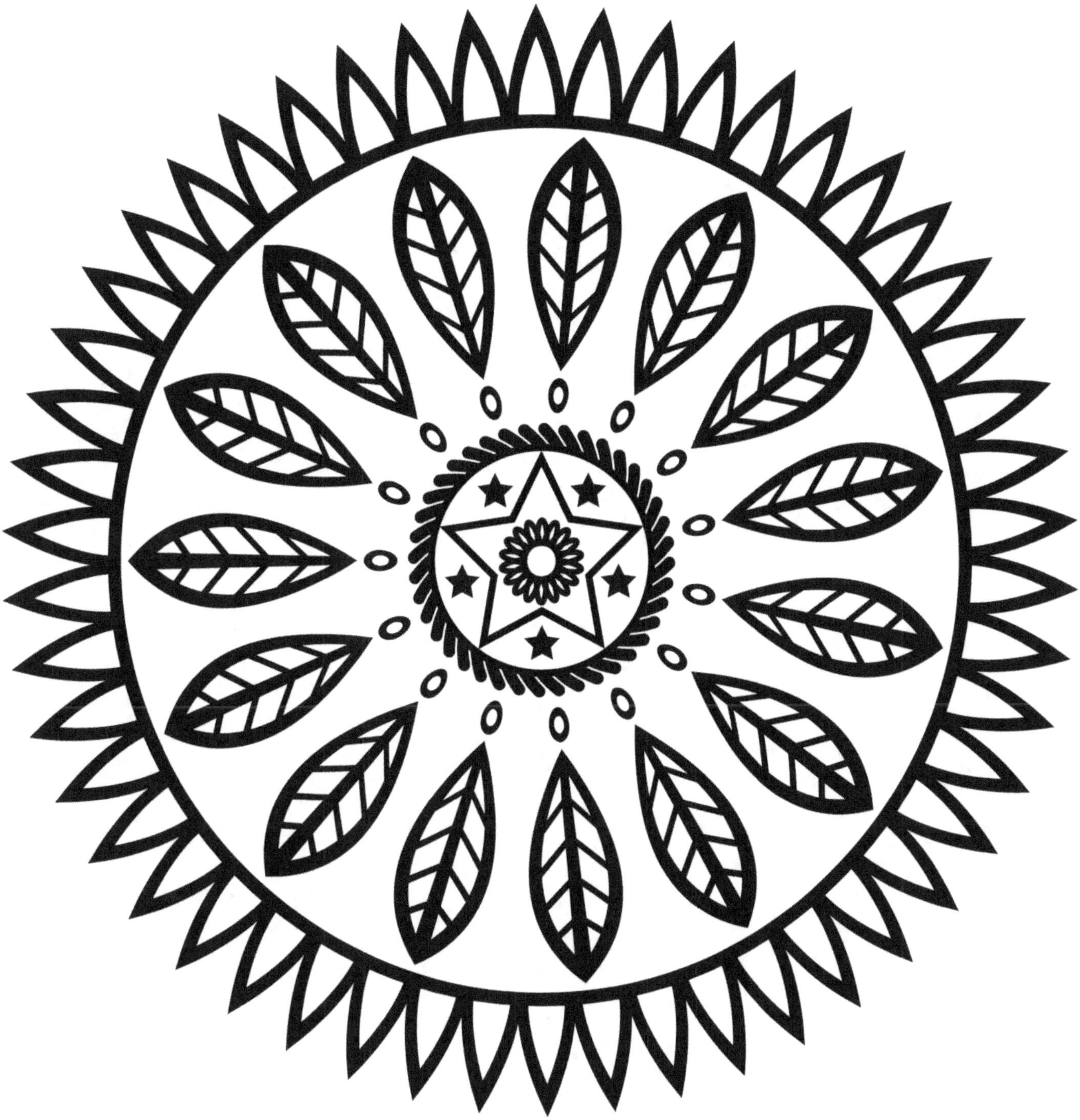

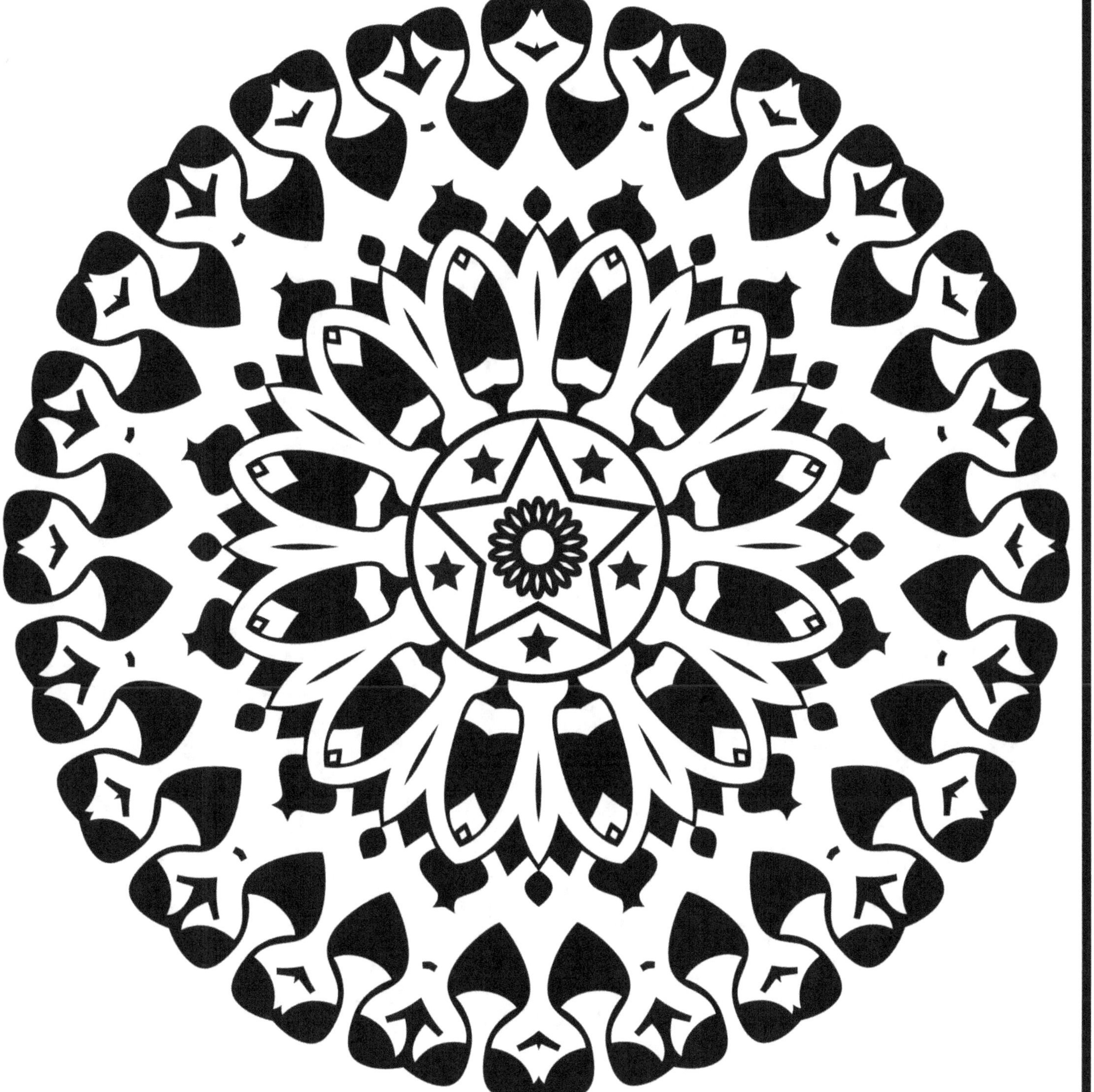

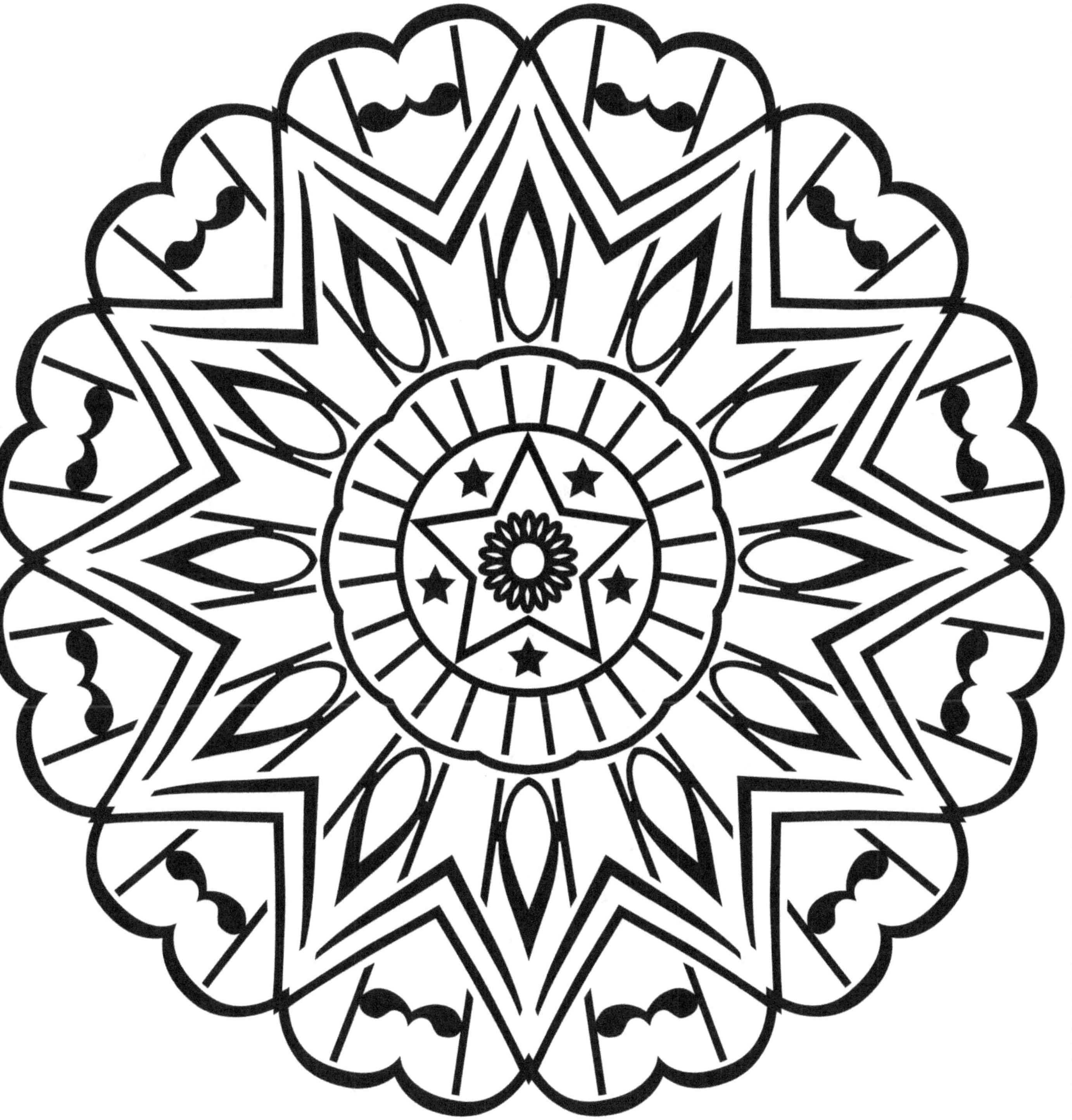

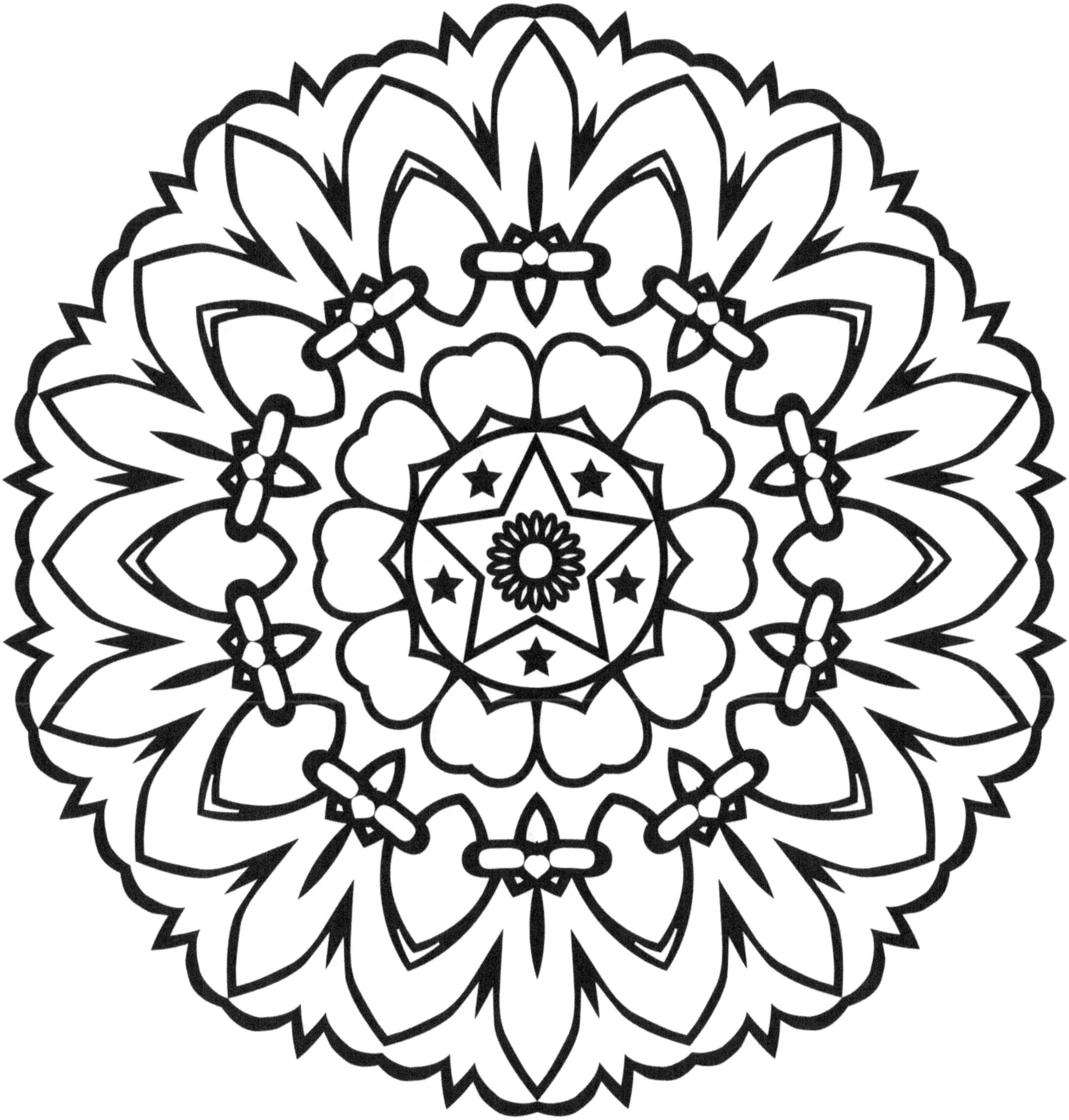

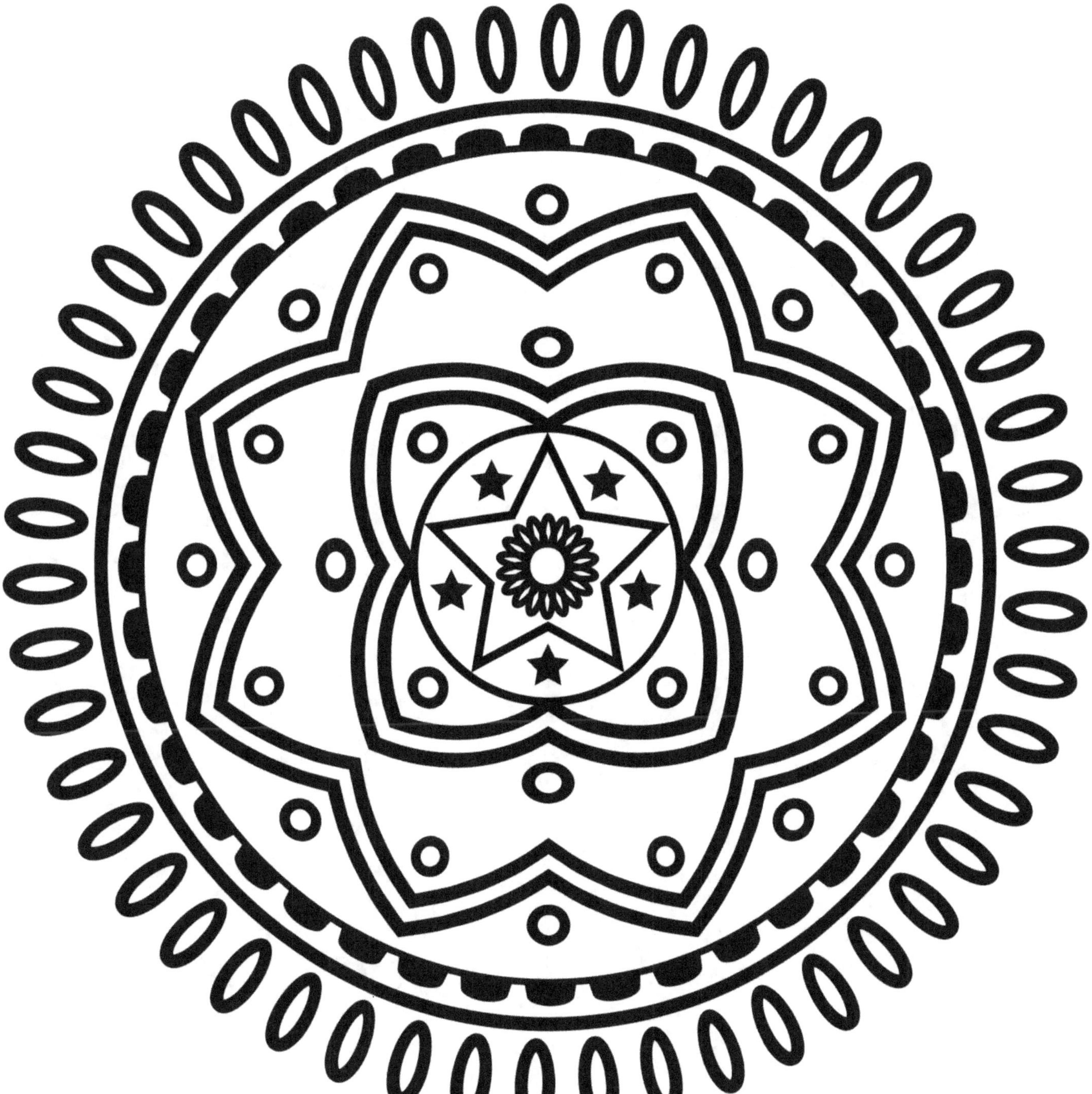

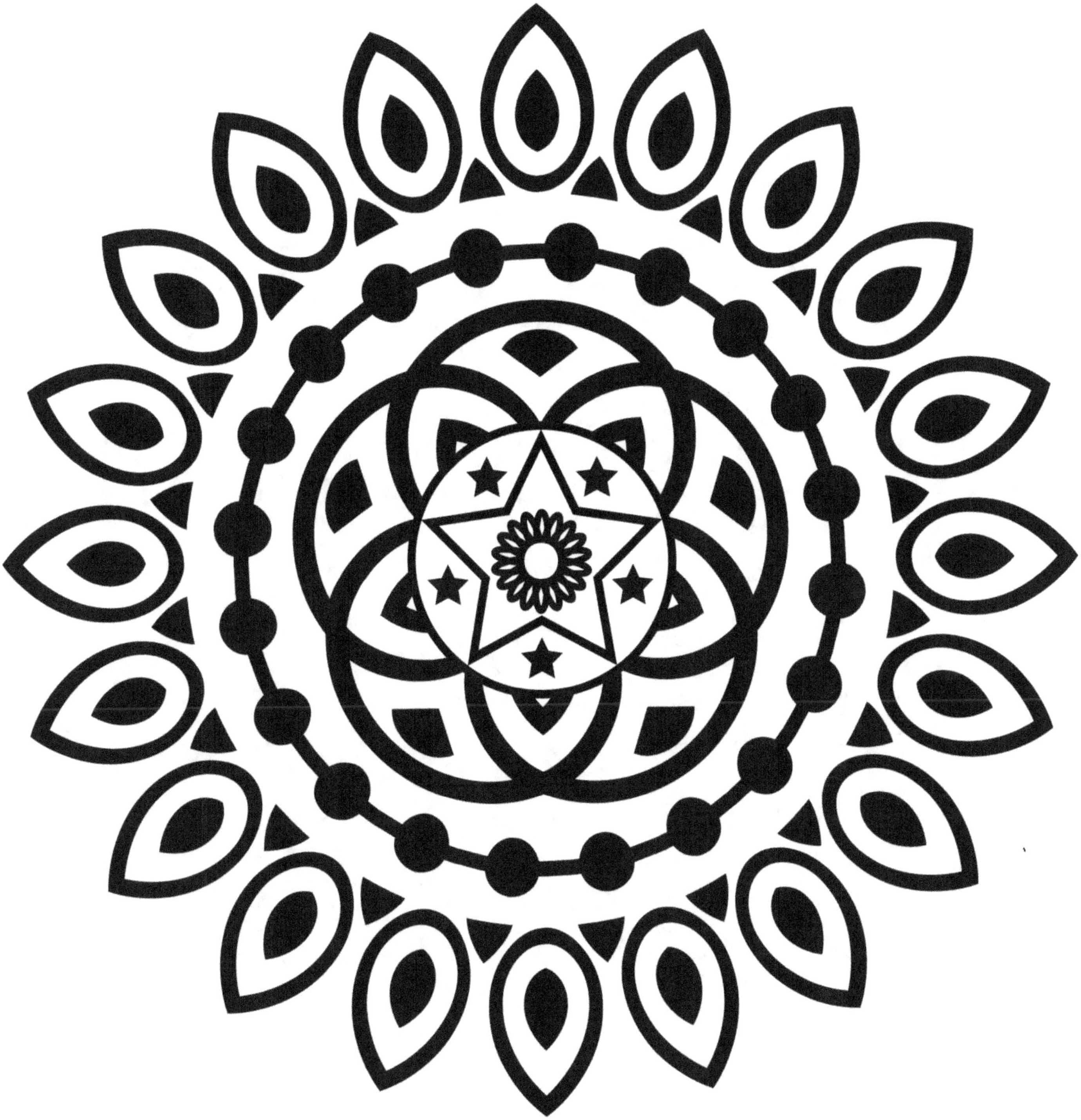

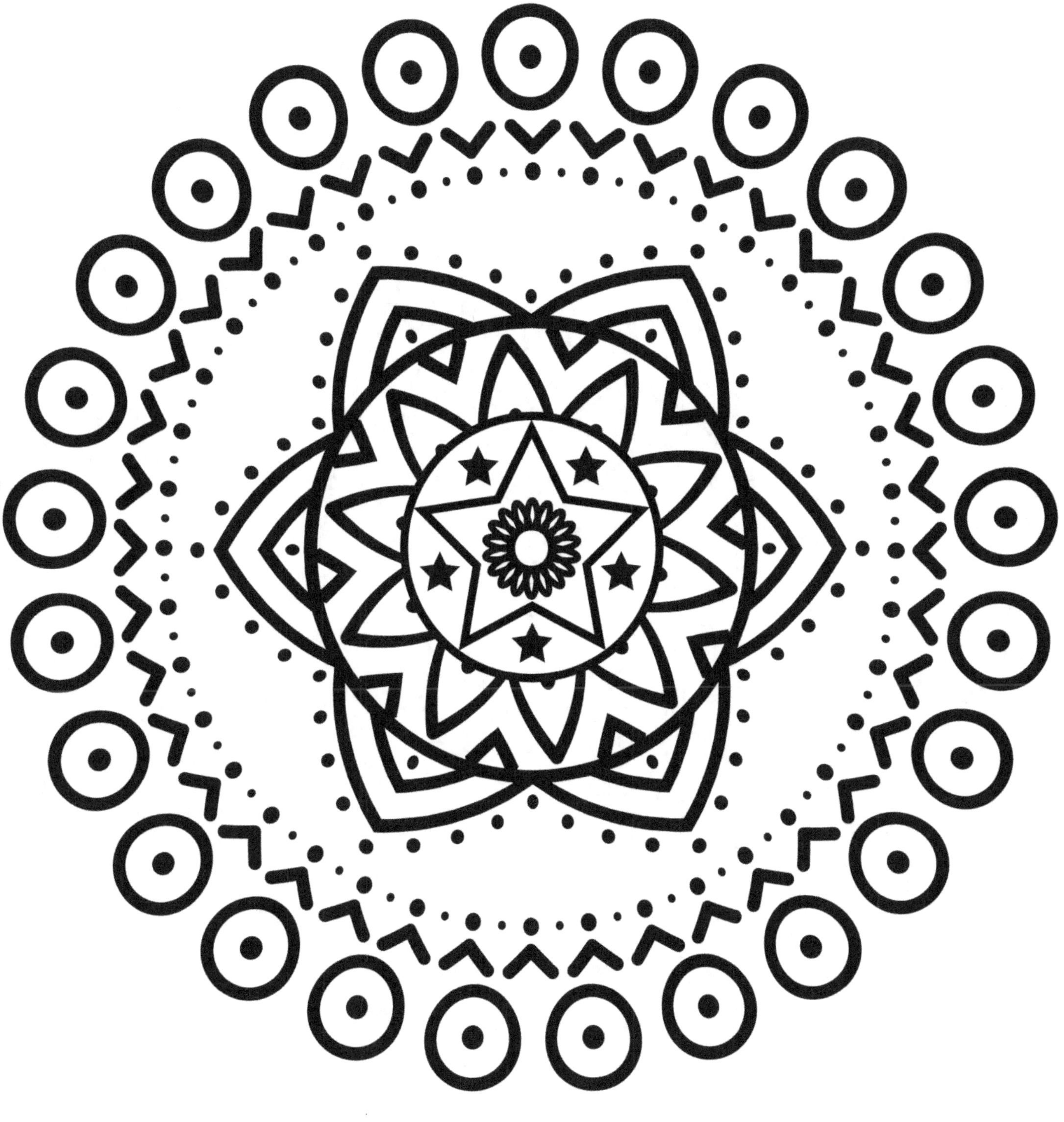

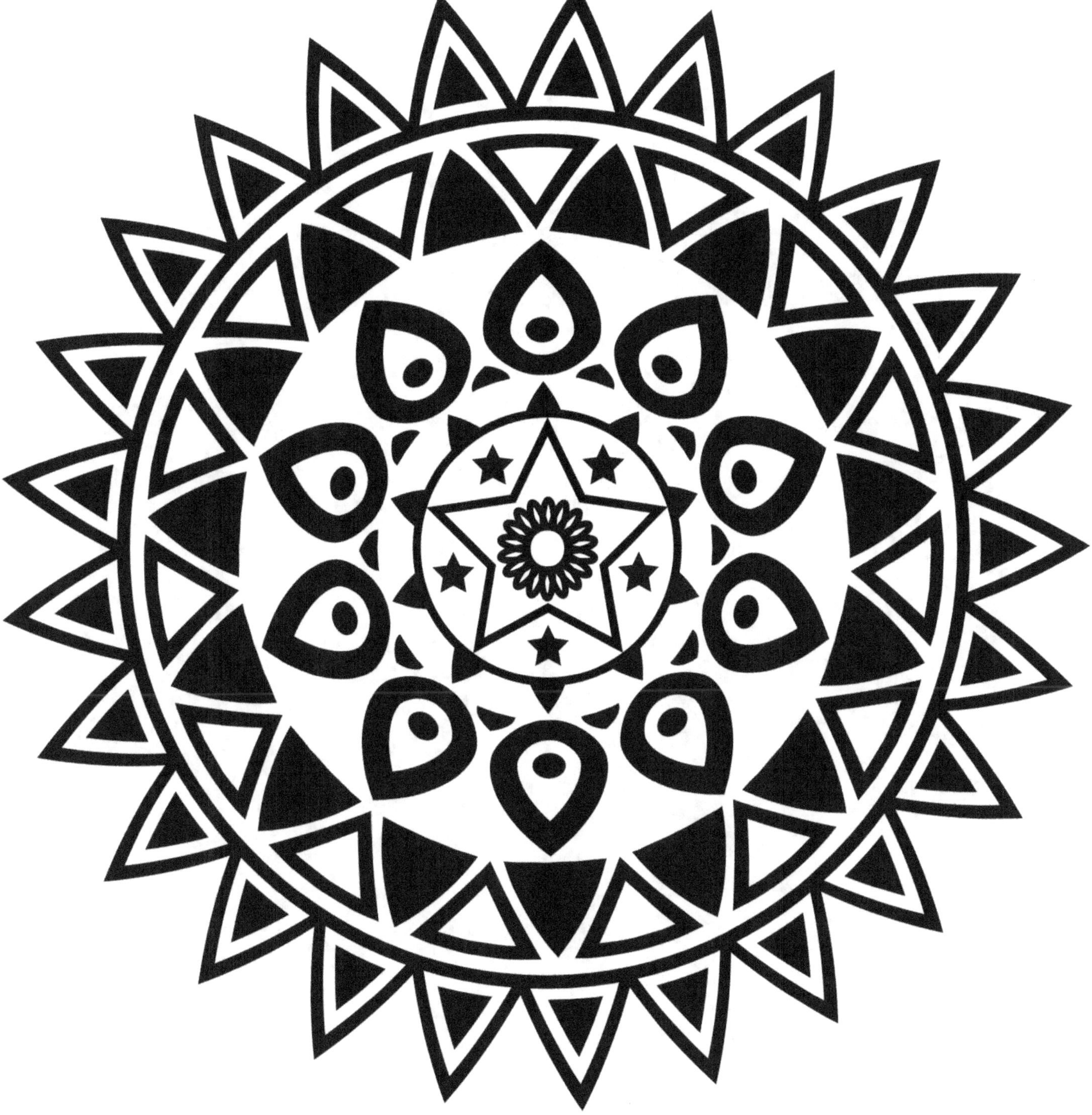

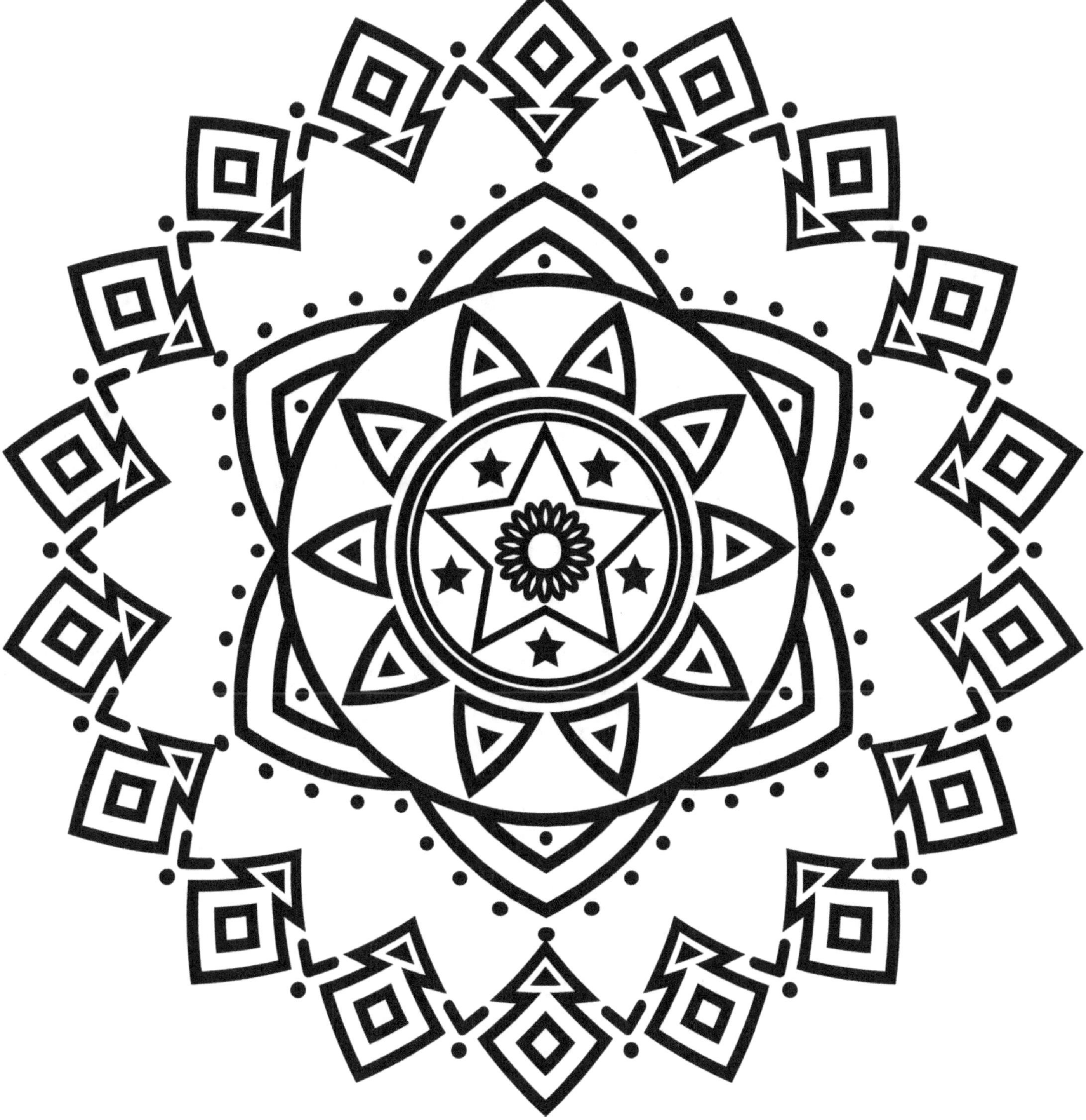

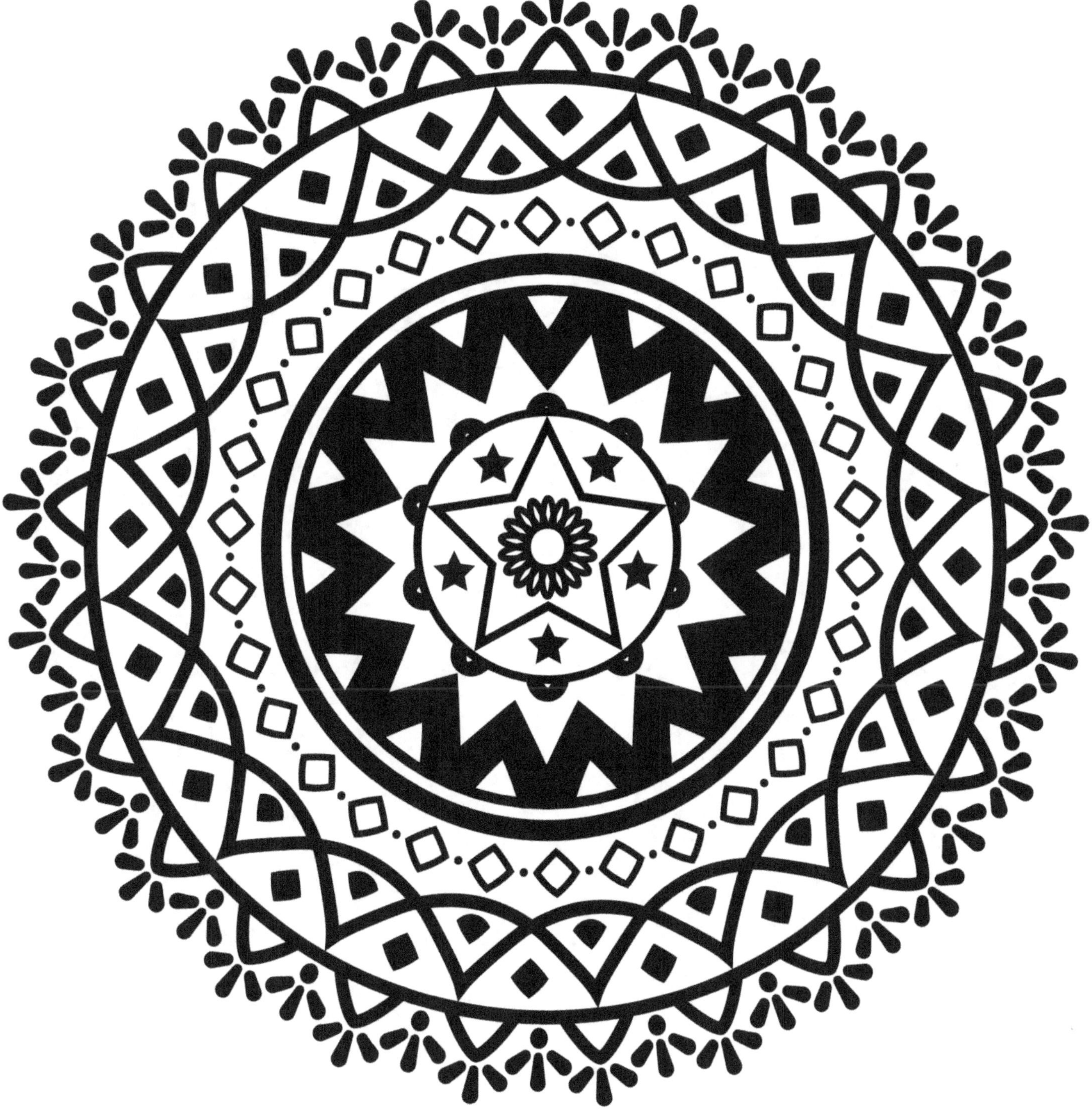

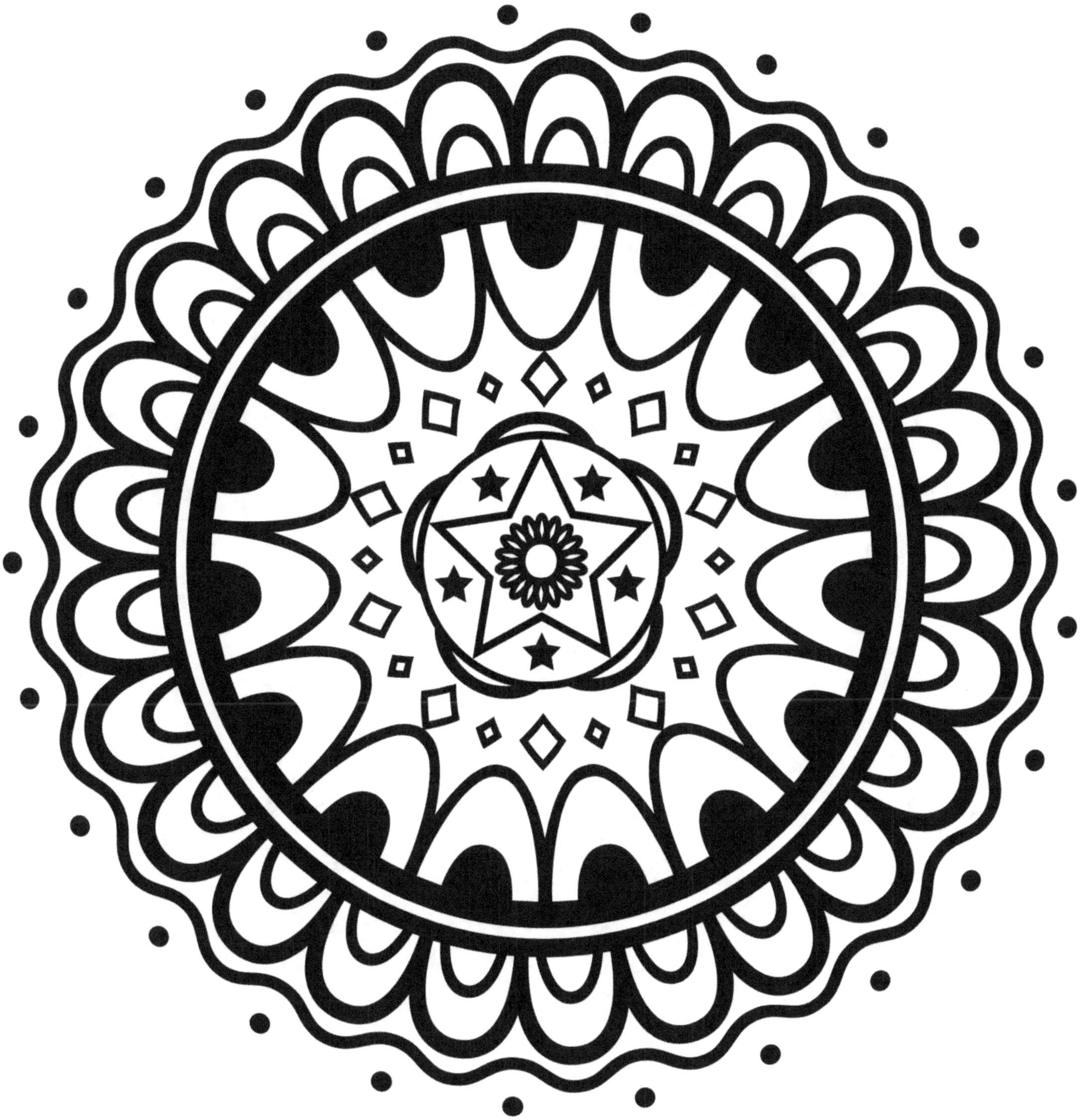

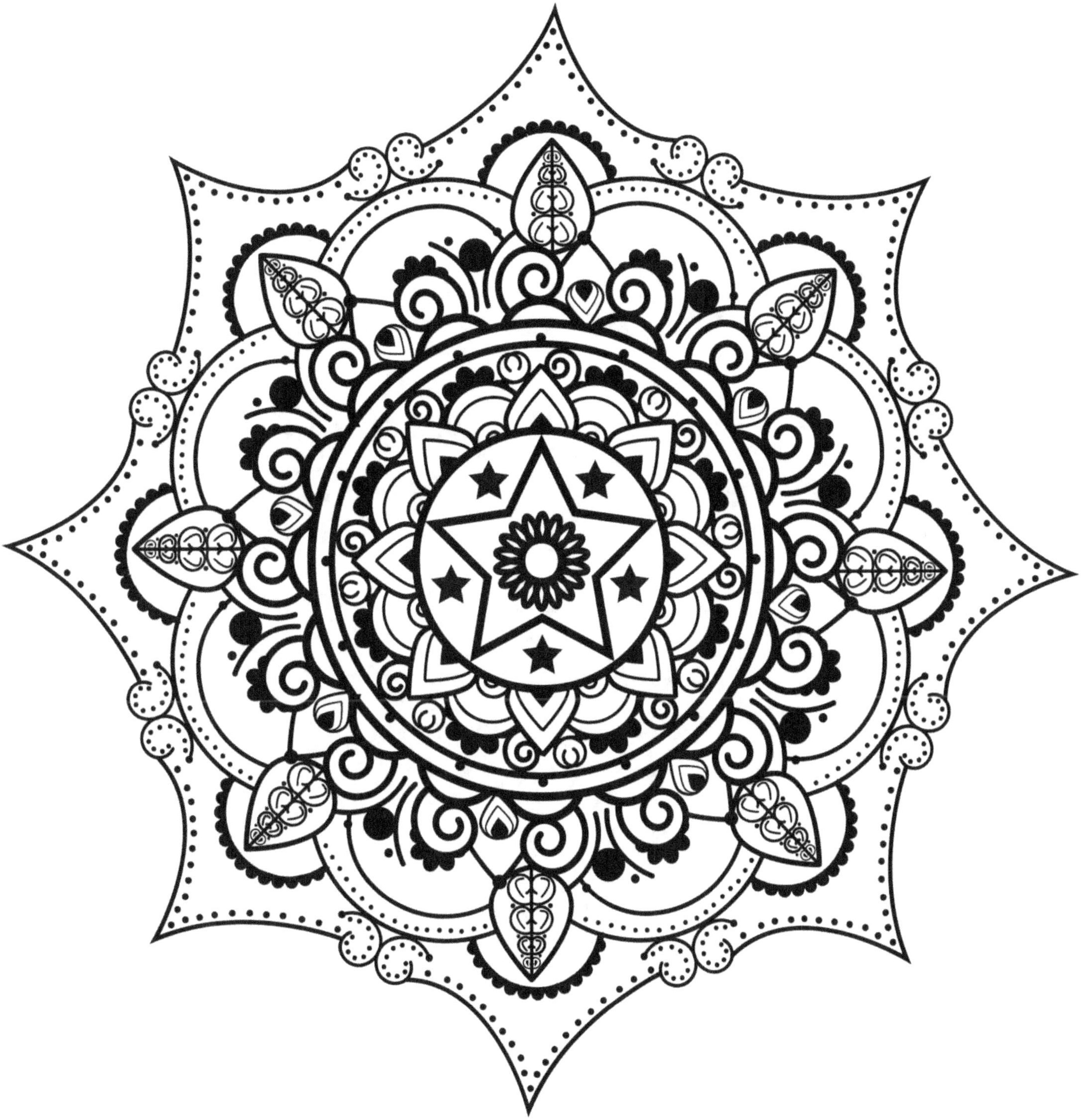

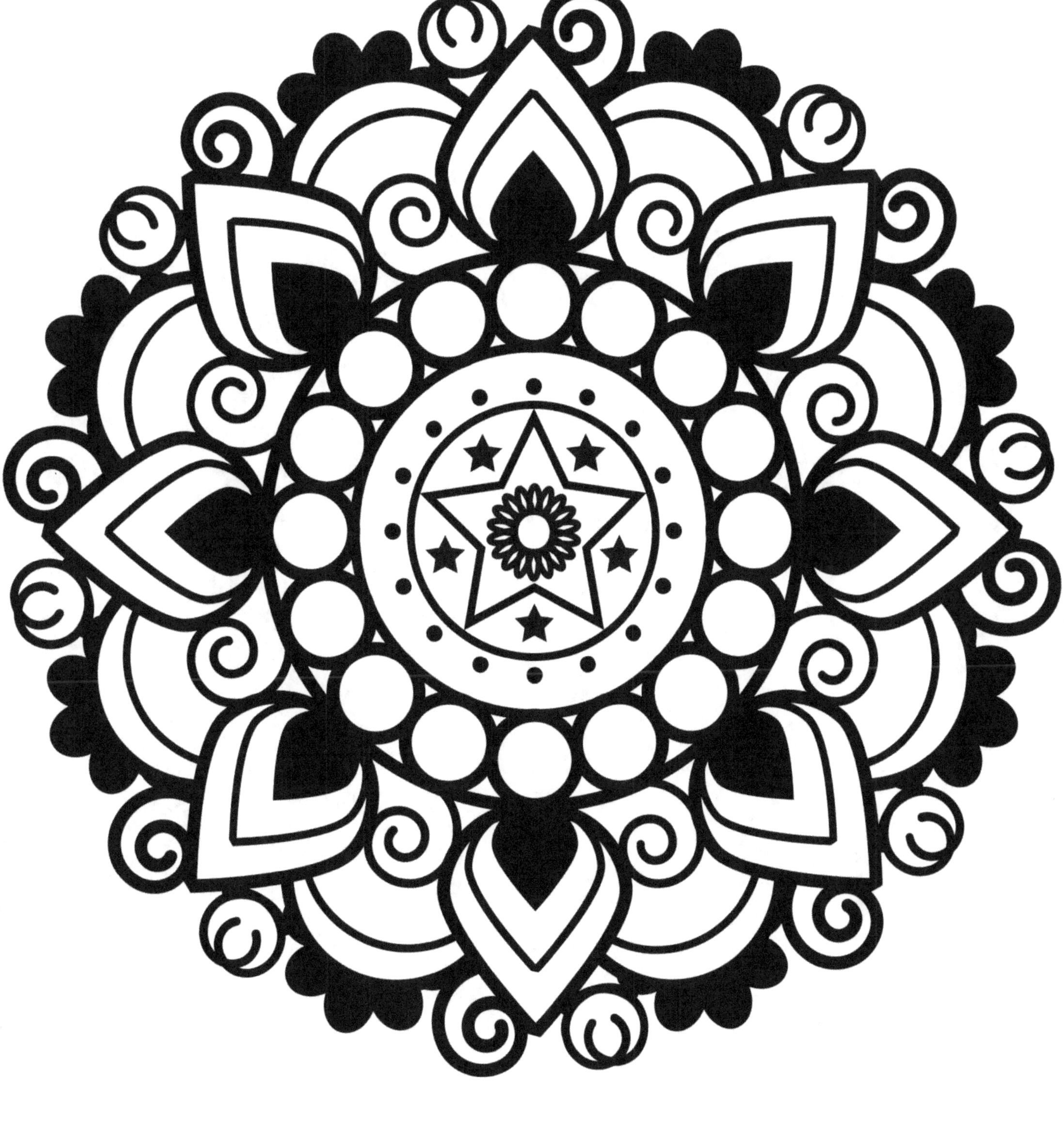

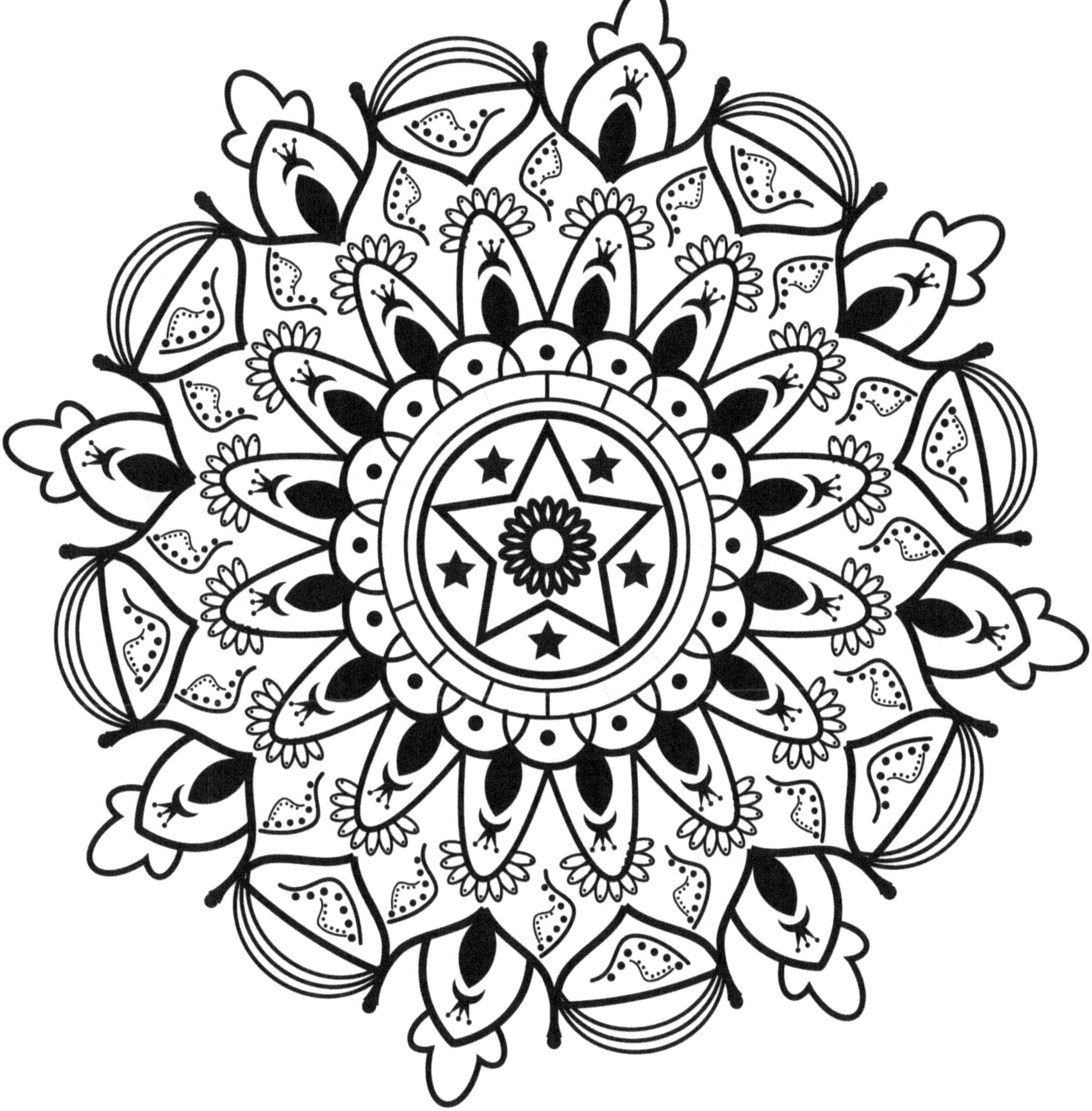

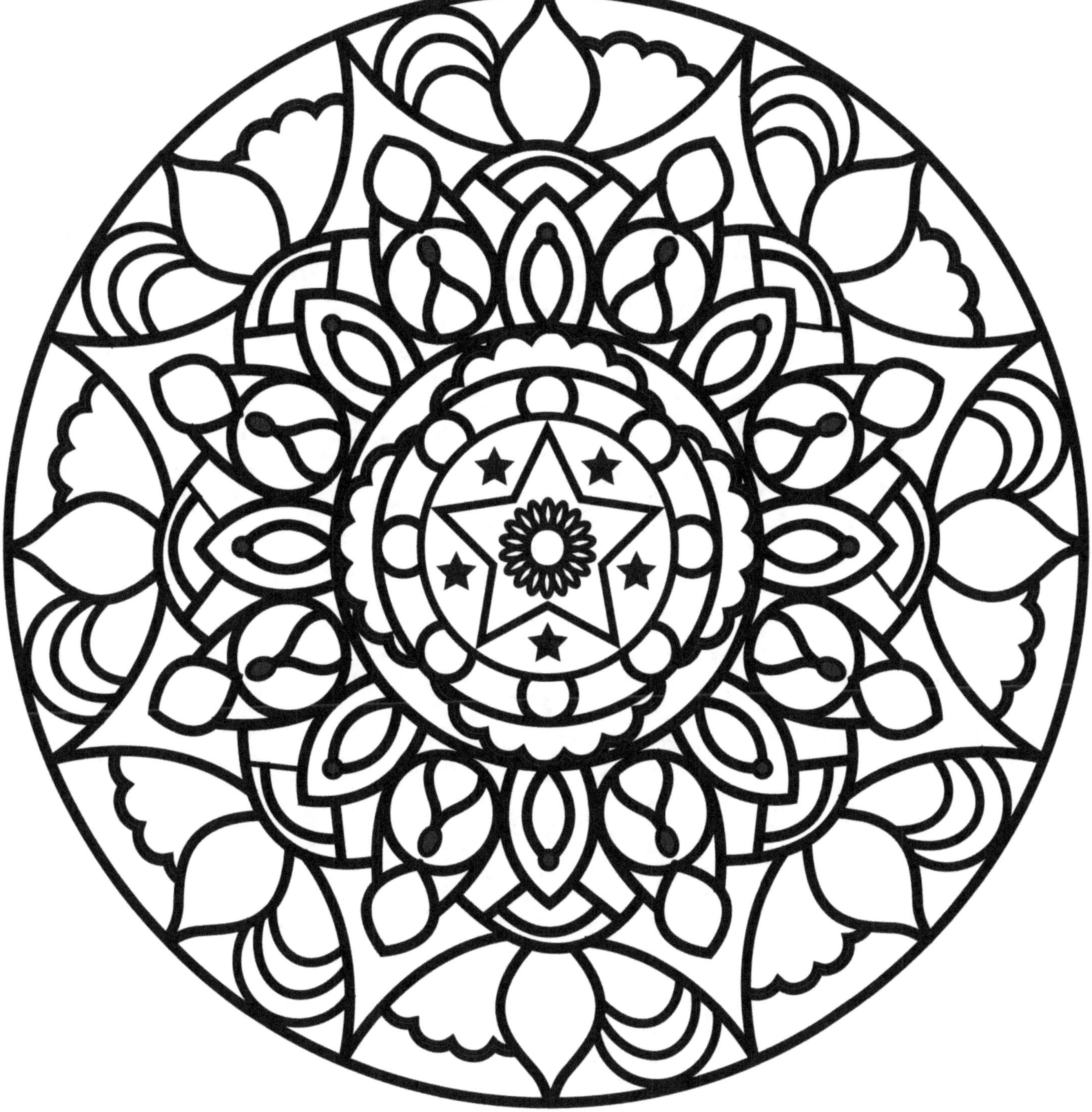

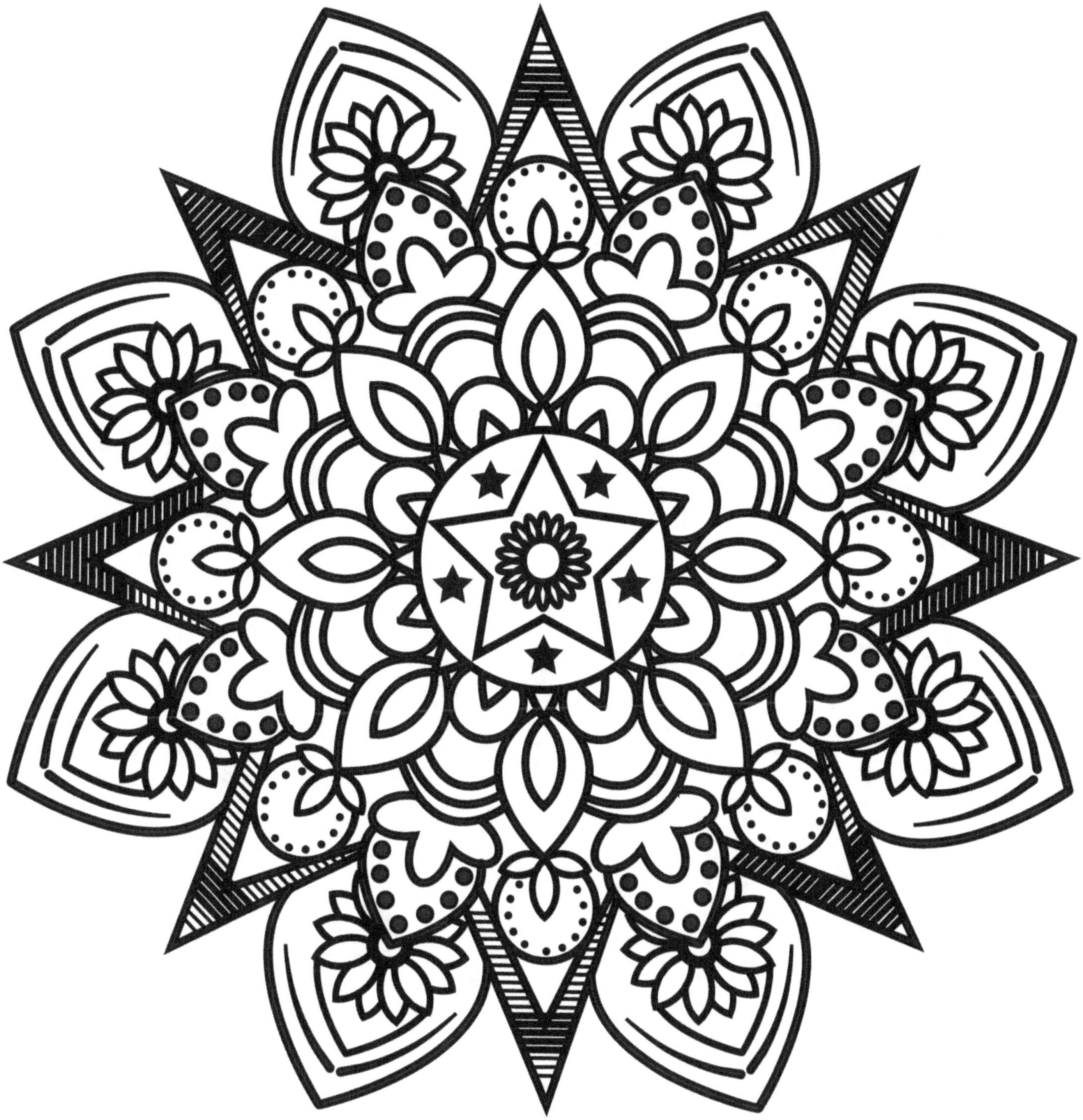

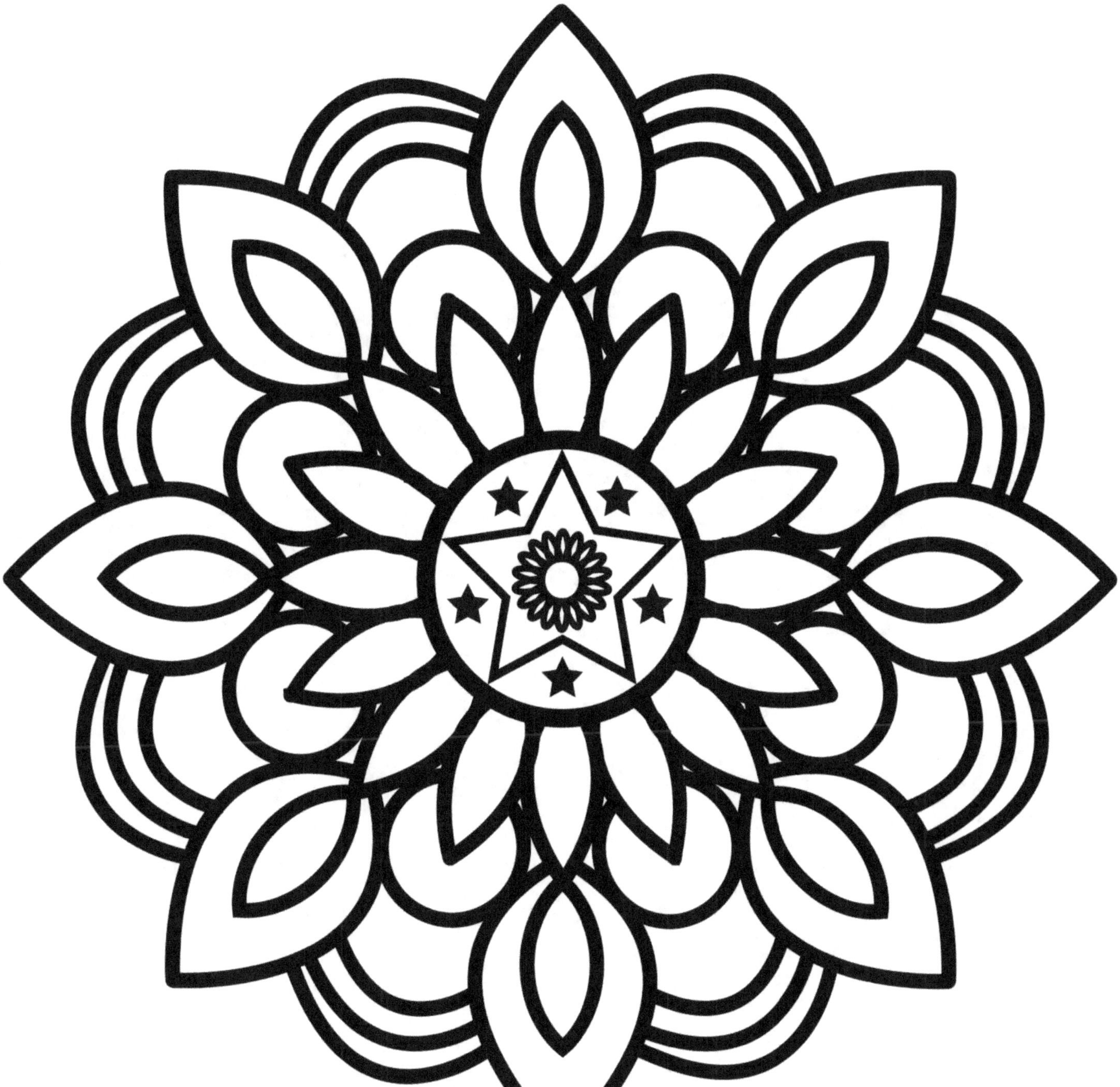

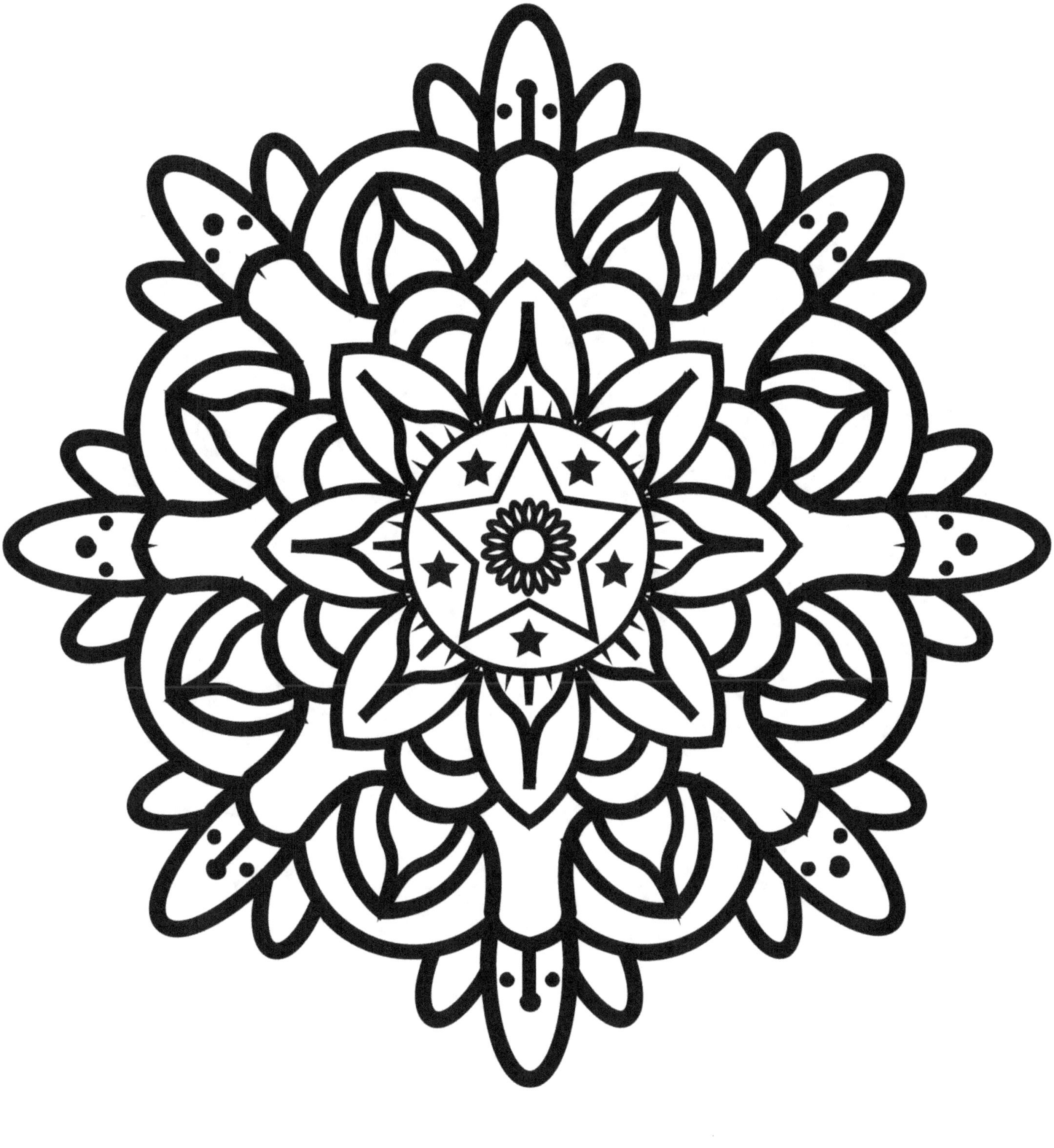

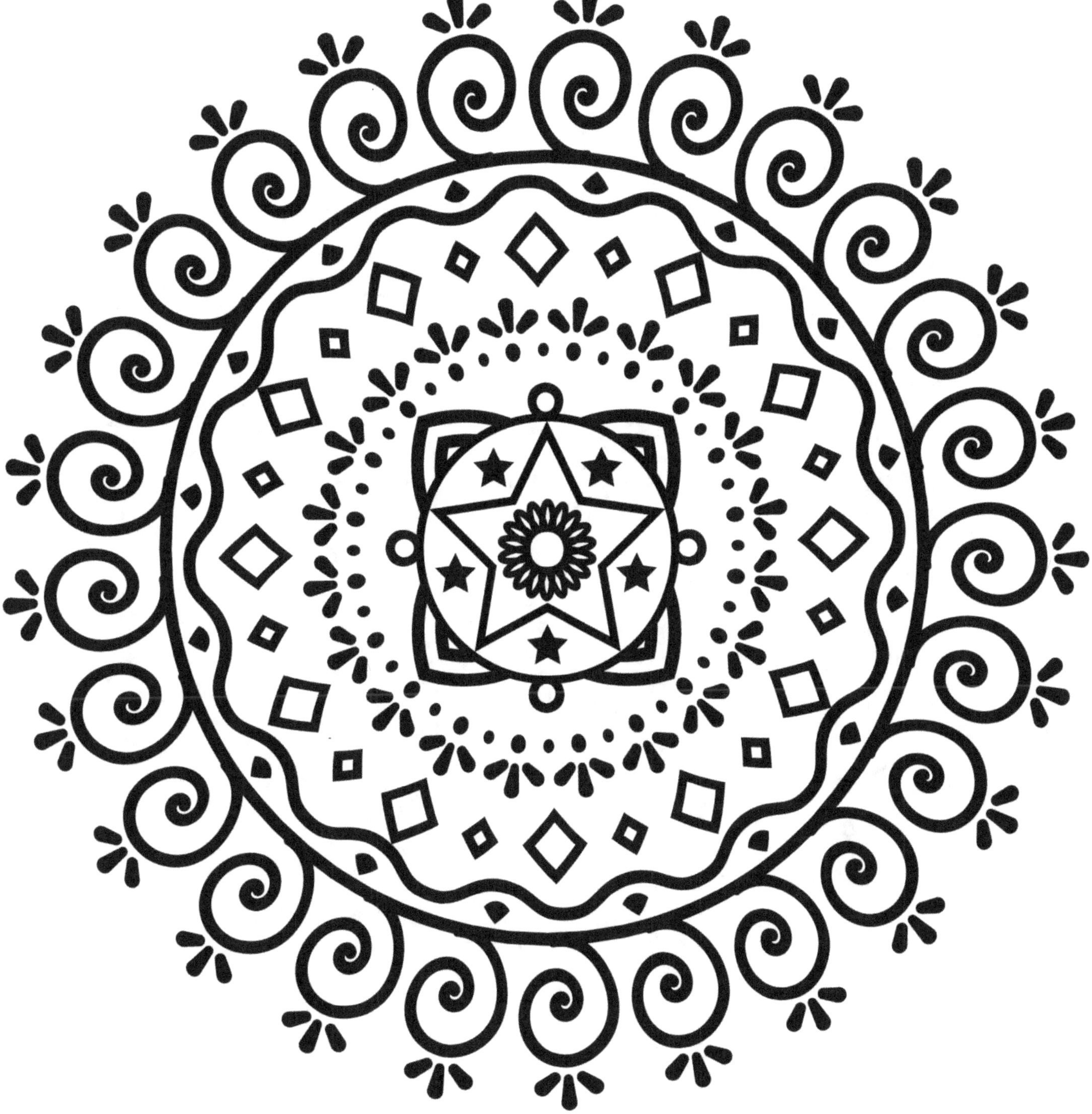

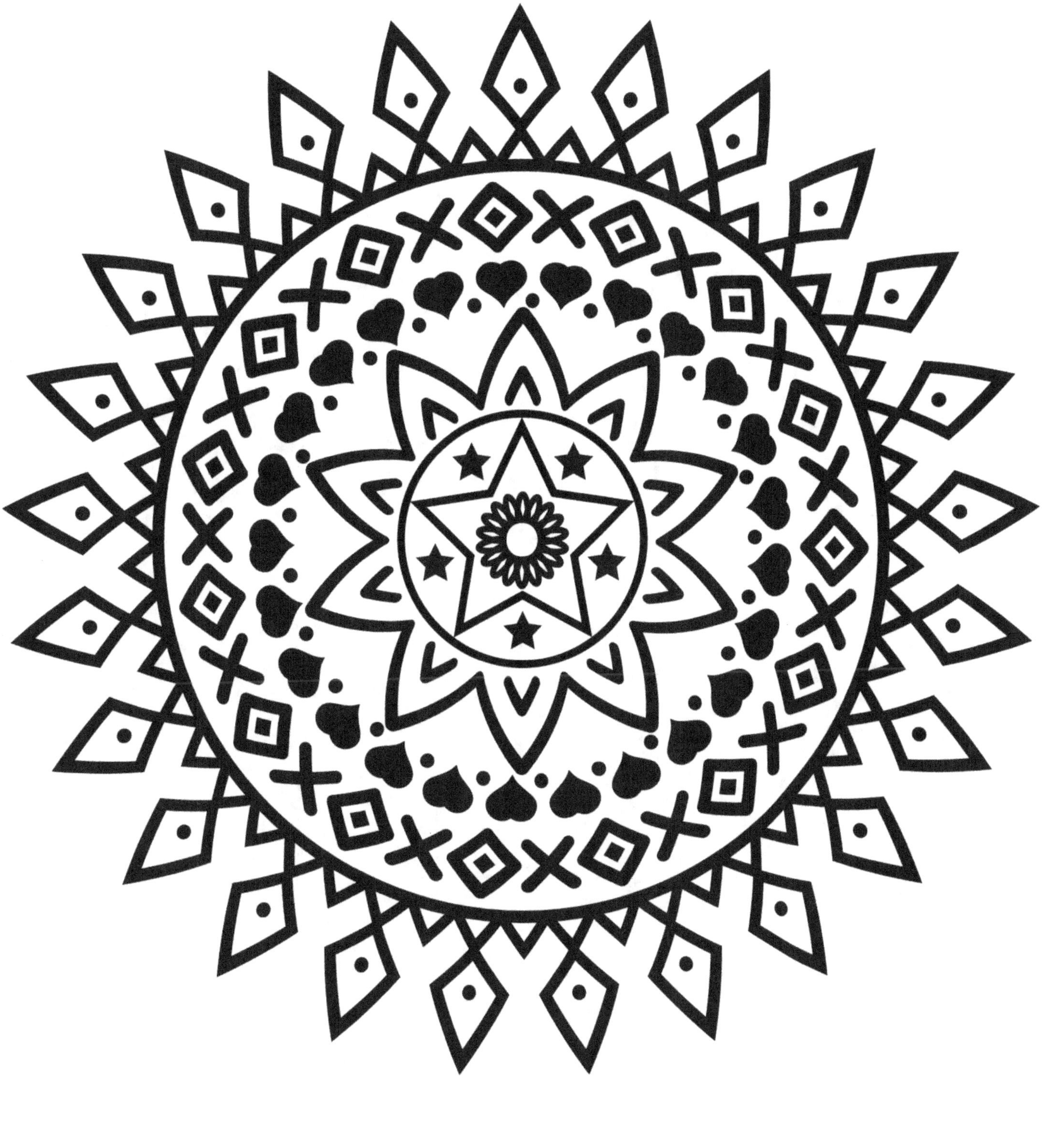

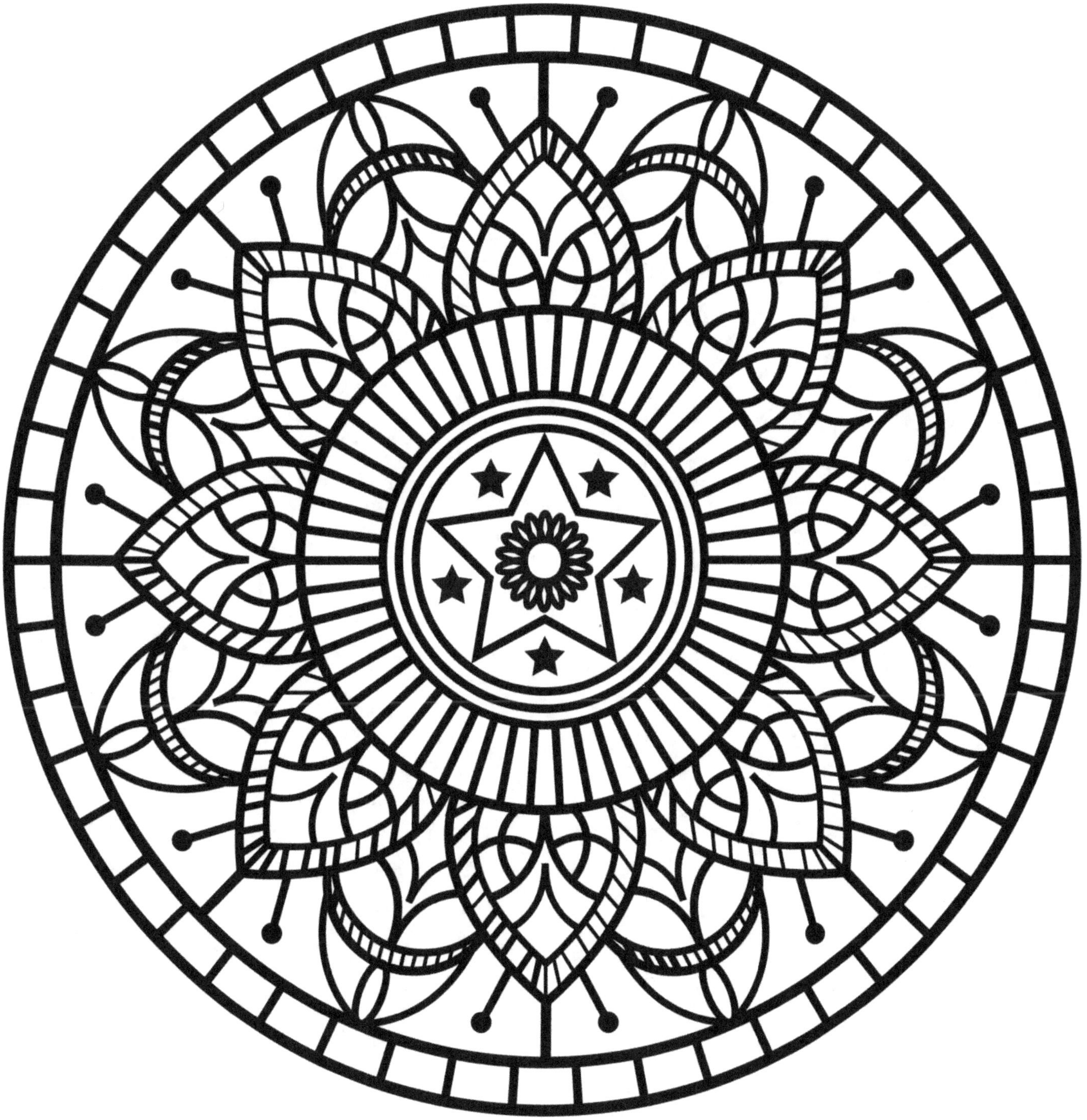

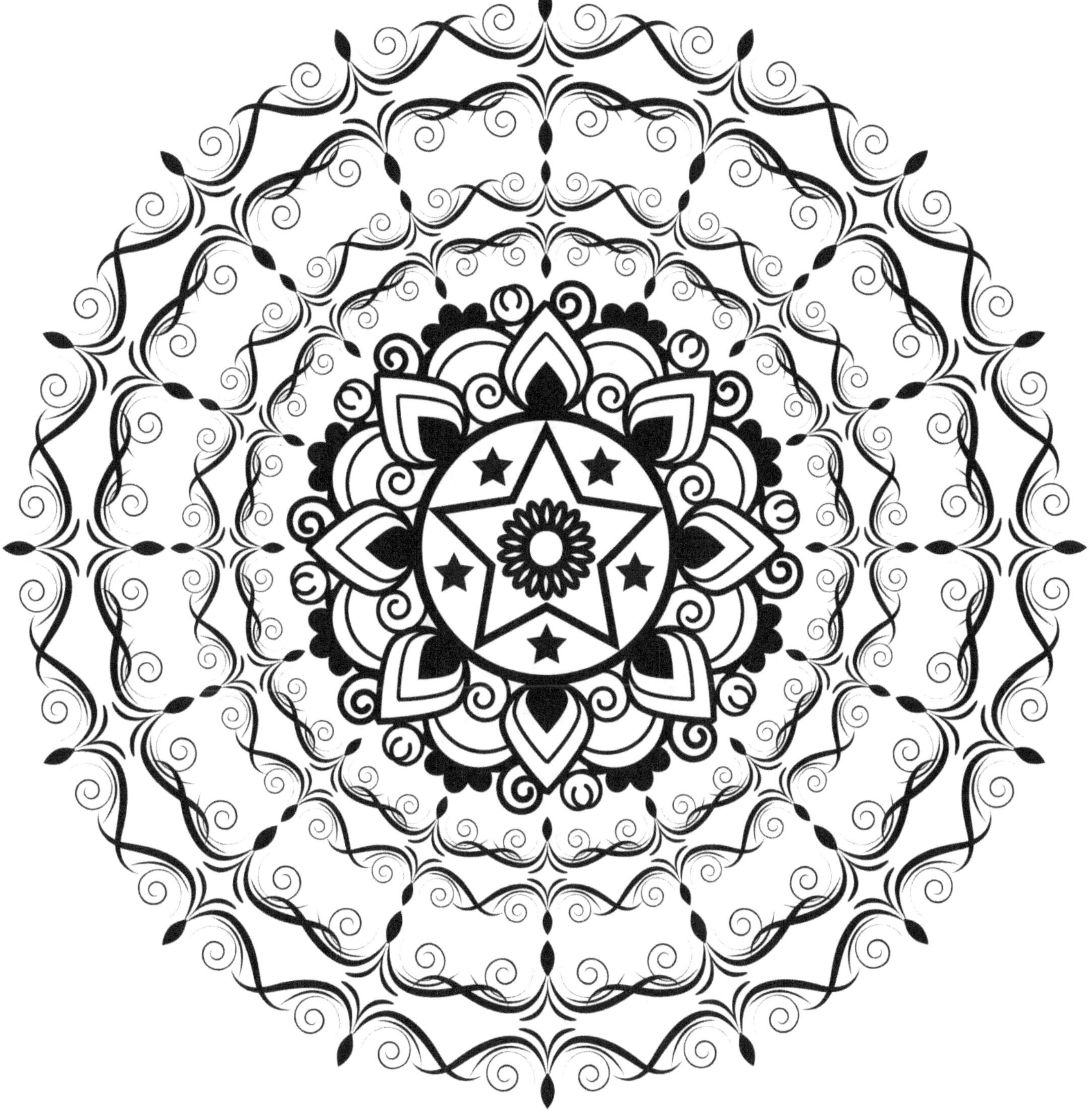

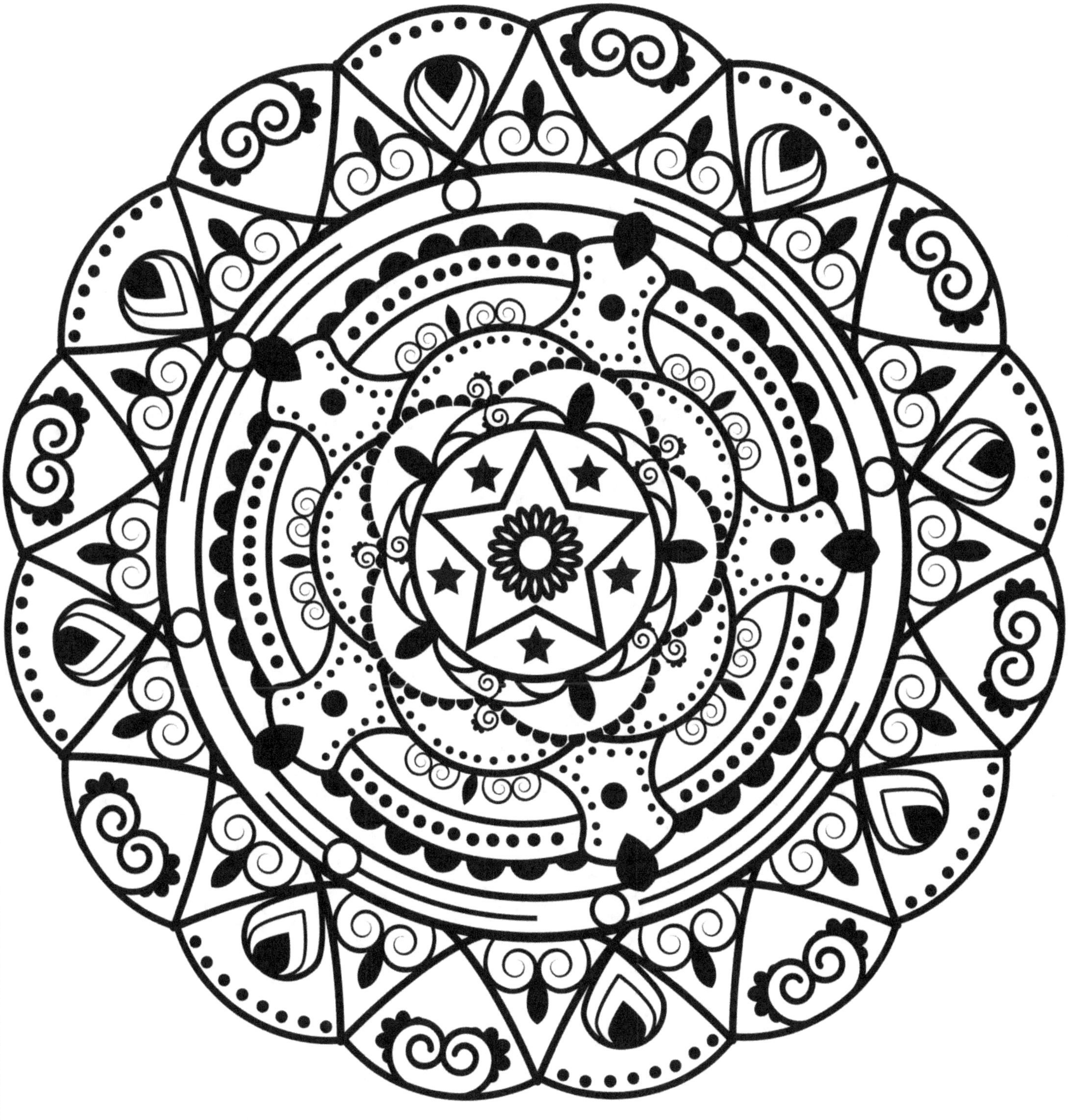

Color Test Page...

Color Test Page...

www.ingramcontent.com/pod-product-compliance
Lightning Source LLC
Chambersburg PA
CBHW082218290526
45794CB00009B/3590